FOOD FAITH *and* FASTING

A Sacred Journey to Better Health

RITA MADDEN, M.P.H., R.D.

ANCIENT FAITH PUBLISHING
CHESTERTON, INDIANA

Food, Faith & Fasting: A Sacred Journey to Better Health

Published by:
Ancient Faith Publishing
A Division of Ancient Faith Ministries
P.O. Box 748
Chesterton, IN 46304

ISBN: 978-1-936270-48-4

Printed in the United States of America

To My Parents

"Always let mercy outweigh everything else in you.
A hard and unmerciful heart will never be pure."
—St. Isaac of Syria

This portrays the love you show me
and everyone you encounter.
The way you live has always been my biggest teacher.

I am eternally grateful for the gift
God has bestowed upon me in you.

CONTENTS

INTRODUCTION

The Focus of This Book

One morning, Chris, a dear friend, discussed with her church-school class the concept of fasting from certain foods. She held up an egg and asked the kindergartners, "Where do eggs come from?" To her surprise, many kids waved their hands and shouted, "Foodland!"

That response startled Chris, for she was expecting to hear "Chickens!" rather than the name of the town's small-chain grocery store.

As I reflect on that incident, I'm still shocked by the children's response. It's a sad reality that I'm starting unwillingly to accept as I see more and more "food products," wrapped in cellophane packaging and neon designs, crowd our grocery-store shelves.

That incident led me to ask, Do these children know the foods of their ancestors? Do they realize foods come in forms other than plastic wrap and boxes? Do they know what the apostles ate? Are they aware that the Creator of all simply spoke and foods came into being to nourish their growing bodies, allowing them to run and play with their friends?

That conversation with Chris was one of many that propelled me to explore what connections might exist between food and faith.

Throughout this book, we will use the grace and wisdom of the Ancient Eastern Orthodox Christian Tradition to take us back to the basics, encouraging us to adopt a rhythm of eating and living that allows us to enjoy food and exercise. Moreover, the rhythm plays a tune for us, guiding us to fast and feast, connecting our care for health to something greater.

We will learn what and how to eat in order to nurture our health and facilitate sensible weight loss. We will work toward forming a healthy relationship with food, approaching eating and health in a way that glorifies our Creator.

This book is for the parents who are trying to feed their families right. It is for the college students who are learning to eat on their own. It is for the single person living alone or with roommates. It is for those who live in monasteries, eating in community and providing hospitality to visitors.

Moreover, the book is written for those who are struggling with the concept of caring for their health in a balanced way. These include (but are not necessarily limited to) the person who tries every new dietary recommendation; the one who is obsessed with, or tyrannized by, rigid eating rules; and the person who has a preoccupation with healthy eating that unwittingly ends up inducing stress in everyday life. Food (and health for that matter) may take such a hold in a person's life that it becomes an idol. The book will address ways of dealing with that idol.

In our culture, the notion of eating for the right reason— that reason being to commune with God— has been lost. Caring for body and soul has become out of balance. The hope is that this book will aid in restoring that balance.

This book is a nutrition-based approach for all ages, ethnicities, genders, and professions. It is for people who wish to care for their health by eating in ways that will deepen their communion with God.

Both those who are new to the Orthodox Tradition and those familiar with the faith will encounter more teachings and practices of the tradition. And those who are immersed in the Orthodox Tradition might find in the book helpful reminders that will reinforce the notion that caring for our health can be an avenue through which we can nurture and deepen our practice in the faith.

Your Commitment

This book is designed to provide you with modern-day practical nutrition guidance, supported by the Orthodox Tradition. I encourage you to make the commitment to read this brief book and implement its exercises within a limited time frame (see below). In fact, it is designed in a way that will guide you to do just that.

Each section provides you with hands-on exercises that will make the discussed concepts a part of your everyday life. The hope is that in a few short weeks you can make health changes to benefit you for a lifetime.

You may wish to read this book in community. Consider starting a small group at your church or hosting one in your home or work setting. Invite other Christians (or people who are open to Christian values) who are trying to better their health through a faith-based approach.

Or you may consider reading this little book with your spouse, family, or a close friend. The instant support and accountability you create in reading alongside others is highly beneficial.

You may also read it on your own, but it's important to try your best to keep yourself on track with the suggested timetable so you can reap the fruits of your labor.

How to Use this Book

Together, we are about to embark on a sacred journey to better health. Let's pack our bags and get ready to go!

- Each chapter is designed with Sections and Training Tools.
- Each section contains a specific topic of discussion.
- Training Tools are found at the end of each section and contain hands-on activities for you to complete.

- Read each section in order and complete the Training Tool activity.
- Don't move to the next chapter until you've completed the hands-on activities associated with the chapter you're on.
- The material in each chapter coincides with and builds upon the previous chapter.
- Set a time frame that works for you to complete this book. (For example, complete a chapter within a week or two weeks.)

And now let our journey begin!

Let's Start Today

In these times of fast-food restaurants and vending machines, it doesn't take a doctor, a scientist, or a food expert to explain to us how we have lost sight of cultural and traditional ways of eating. Our contemporary lifestyle demands instant gratification and an ability to shop online for virtually anything. Like a giant tidal wave, this lifestyle has engulfed and scattered us.

We've lost the focus and awareness that make our faith the definitive guide and anchor when it comes to living and caring for our health. My hope is that the teachings of the Orthodox Tradition, accompanied by the modern-day health guidelines presented in this book, will aid us in recovering those aspects of our faith that steer us to a balanced relationship in wellness.

I thank God and Ancient Faith Publishing for giving me the opportunity to share with you this modern-day yet age-old information. Throughout this book, I mention some personal observations relating to sound health and nutrition practices, observations that tap into and reflect the wisdom of many saints, early Church Fathers, and present-day spiritual fathers and mothers who are part of the Orthodox Tradition. Now let the fasting to better health begin!

At this point it is important to state the following disclaimer:

The information presented in this book does not outline a cure for specific medical conditions, but it does provide some guidance for health and nutrition practices. I hope and pray that this information will be beneficial for your life in the areas of proper eating and healthy faith-based living.

CHAPTER ONE

Sacred Eating

"What is the purpose of life?" This question has engaged the thinking of philosophers, theologians, and many other individuals throughout history.

Saint Athanasius, one of the early Church Fathers, tells us, "God became man so that men might become gods." Now, we might say, "Become a god—a god? That's our purpose? Um, okay—no pressure!"

Seriously, how do we understand this significant insight? Through the Orthodox Tradition, we understand that God wants us to partake in Him. Our goal, our purpose, our reason for being is what the Greek language refers to as *theosis*: attainment, likeness, illumination, or union with God.

> *Man has been ordered to become God.*
>
> —St. Gregory of Nazianzus

Humans can—and should—work to attain union with God. God desires this. He wants to adopt us into His Kingdom, making everything that is His ours. He created us to share in His Divinity and yearns for us to come home.

Working toward theosis allows us to become co-workers with God. We choose to participate in the continual work of sharing love. Put simply, theosis connects us to God, who is love; therefore our true nature is partaking of love and, by extension, becoming vessels of love.

We have fallen away from our true nature, and our soul longs to go home. We need a road map to get back there. The Orthodox Tradition provides us with that map, helping us return to our divine state, our everlasting home.

Caring for Our Health as a Spiritual Act

Does caring for our health fit into this purpose of theosis, and if so, how? Saint Maximos the Confessor (fourth century), Saint Gregory of Palamas (fourteenth century), and many other saints throughout history have affirmed that man being made in God's image is body and soul, and they interact to ascend toward God.

> *Man as God's image is body and soul, and they interact and ascend toward God.*
>
> —St. Gregory Palamas

If our purpose in this earthly life is to attain union with God, then it is essential to understand that this does *not* entail a separation of our body and soul. It is *not* just our soul that is working on connecting with God while our body hangs around twiddling its thumbs. It is both soul *and* body that work together to achieve our life's purpose.

The Orthodox Tradition embodies a purification process that has been passed down to us through the ages. This is where we come to understand what ascetical practices in the Orthodox Tradition are all about. *Asceticism* translated from the Greek means "exercise" or "training."

The ascetical practices that have been passed down to us include love, humility, prayer, silence, fasting, and self-control. These disciplines are a means to an end—the end being that we become fully united and restored to God.

Ascetical practices of Orthodox Tradition include:

* Love
* Humility
* Prayer
* Silence
* Fasting
* Self-control

These ancient practices are still available to us. We are able to connect with them and use them daily. Indeed, they are the tools that aid us in completing our purpose on earth.

To quote Saint Athanasius again, "For He was made man that we might be made God." Becoming like God is a continuous process, not some kit we order, apply, and then discard. Through grace and the practice of ascetical tradition, we can achieve theosis: the constant being with—and in—the Holy Spirit. It is the path that returns us to the true nature God intended for us.

Today we start. We want to begin by applying these ancient ascetical practices as a means to care for our modern-day health. These practices were here long before we were, and they will be here long after we're gone. This approach has stood the test of time, and countless saints have received illumination by means of it.

At one point these saints were ordinary people like the rest of us, but they pursued the purification process that encompasses these ascetical practices, leading many saints to abide constantly in their Creator.

Now on to the path of purification we go.

We Need to Change

Often when I'm conducting family-nutrition counseling sessions, I get free entertainment by observing those family members who know everyone else's nutrition and health issues but have cloudy vision when it comes to their own. I'll hear one say, "He snacks way too much"; another adds, "She doesn't exercise enough." Like a ping-pong ball, my head goes back and forth, listening to the loving "I-have-no-issues-of-my-own" banter.

Of course, we all know and have heard it over and over again: No one is perfect. Not Dr. X, not talk-show host Y or supermodel Z. We all eat; we all need to eat. We all sleep; we all need to sleep. We all breathe—and so forth.

We all are in need of change: change of heart, change of

mind, change of diet, change of lifestyle. As stated earlier, becoming like God is a continuous process. So let the change begin.

The early Holy Fathers of the Orthodox Tradition frequently note that change starts with *metanoia*, a Greek word from which the English word "repentance" was derived. *Metanoia* is defined as a complete change of mind, doing a 180-degree turn, as it were, and turning completely away from an old action.

This is how we need to appreciate the word *repentance* when we hear it in church. Unfortunately, many interpret repentance as a negative thing, but we should embrace it in a positive light. It's the start of a strong desire to change. We need to be energized by the rewards of change.

> *If there is no struggle,*
> *there is no progress.*
> —Frederick Douglass

Through true repentance we choose to free ourselves of our old bad habits and commit to making a change for the new. We make the choice to "clean house." We get rid of what we do not want to do anymore. We identify where we have fallen and come to understand that our chosen actions have distanced us from our Creator.

Then we make a plan to try *not* to fall into the same action again. This sounds good and easy, but the reality, as we well know, is that we're going to fall. But what should we do when we fall? That's right: get back up. That's our intention: to rise up and draw nearer to our Creator.

My hope and prayer is that this little book is going to provide us with some strategies to help us decrease the number and severity of our falls. The book's thrust grapples with this concept: Failing to care for our health is a way to distance ourselves from our Creator. Or to put it more positively: Caring for our health can—and should—be an edifying component of our faith.

The Road to Better Health

"Habit is a difficult thing: it is hard to break and hard to avoid," Saint John Chrysostom notes. "Therefore, the more you understand the power of a habit, the more should you endeavor to be rid of a bad habit and adopt a good one."

Repentance with a capital R is the first step to developing a good habit. Let us clean out the old and bring in the new. The plan we set up to turn away from our old habit and develop a complete change of mind will be different for each of us, depending on our individual struggles.

So for now, let's think about our health. Let's take some time to think about what we need to change.

> *To improve is to change; to be perfect is to change often.*
> —Winston Churchill

Of course, if this were a nice and easy fix, we could stop reading this book right now and be on our merry way to a healthier life. The Holy Fathers emphasize that moving away from our bad habits is not going to happen without a struggle or effort. They explain we are going to be competing against our passions in the flesh.

Many of us think of *passion* as something we should desire. If we are passionate about something, it means we are driven to seek it. Yet the meaning of the word *passion* in the early Church was different: it meant "to suffer." Thus, when we refer to *passions* in an Orthodox sense, we are referring to actions that cause us to suffer as they distance us from God.

Gluttony, greed, lust, pride, anger—these are examples of our passions in the flesh. Even though indulging our passions might feel pleasurable, we must contend against them as they are roadblocks in our way to deepening our unity with God.

Freeing ourselves of these worldly desires helps us to empty ourselves, allowing us to make room for Christ in our lives. The harsh reality is that we will be struggling against the evil one and his demons and crafty darts. The demons will constantly tempt us and may even try to lead us into an unhealthy relationship with food.

> *Only struggle a little more. Carry your cross without complaining. Don't think you are anything special. Don't justify your sins and weaknesses, but see yourself as you really are. And, especially, love one another.*
>
> —Father Seraphim Rose

If the evil one sees us working toward attaining theosis—and this can come in the form of bettering our health for the right reasons—then he may try to trip us. For as much as God desires theosis for us, the evil one despises this for us. It seems safe to say that the Holy Fathers would, with one voice, boldly tell us, "There is no magic pill. Don't fall for the diet gimmicks!"

Let's get ready to work and attain the fruits of our labor.

SECTION 1

Let's Practice Sacred Eating

To begin, we'll work on areas that will help us start to form a healthy relationship with food. Let's start by returning to the sacredness of eating.

To do this, we must consider two types of eating behaviors that may sabotage our approach to a sacred relationship with food: one, a lack of attentiveness to eating; and two (and this may sound like a paradox), an unhealthy obsession with healthy eating. Now let's explore each behavior.

A Lack of Attentiveness to Eating

"Mindless eating" is a term coined by the food psychologist Dr. Brian Wansink. This term encompasses many aspects of eating for the wrong reasons. It means not paying sufficient attention to *what* we eat, *why* we eat, and *how much* we eat.

To start handling this issue with food, we might do well to cultivate a practice in Orthodoxy known as *nepsis* or inner attention. Nepsis is the practice of being attentive to the inner workings of our heart and mind. This is somewhat similar to what many today refer to as "mindfulness." Nepsis keeps us alert and awake to our thoughts and actions.

Tito Colliander, a twentieth-century Finnish Eastern Orthodox writer, offers this analogy to illustrate the importance of nepsis: "The impulse knocks like a salesman at the door. If one lets him in, he begins his sales talk about his wares, and it is hard to get rid of him even if one observes that his wares are not good. Thus follows consent and finally the purchase, often against one's own will."[1]

> *Since I have started becoming more aware of my reasons for eating and making an effort to pray before and after mealtime, I have noticed a six-pound weight loss without even trying. I simply attribute it to being more attentive to why and how I'm eating.*
>
> —Kevin A.

Watchfulness, when it comes to our thoughts and actions, allows us to get in touch with what is best for our soul and body. It is a sort of monitoring device, assisting us not to give in to our passions. St. Gregory the Sinaite teaches us, "Negligence (inattentiveness), like a dark night, kills the soul."[2] We need to be vigilant at all times.

Here is another example from the Orthodox Tradition that illustrates the importance of being watchful in how we deal with our thoughts:

> Two pilgrims once asked an ascetic monk of Mt. Athos, "To what extent are we responsible for the thoughts that attack our intellect?"
>
> The Elder replied, "Airplanes pass over where I live. I cannot hinder the airplanes. I'm not responsible for that. I would be responsible if I began to build an airport. The acceptance of the attacks, which is consent, can be compared to the airport."[3]

Watchfulness, nepsis, helps us to practice mindfulness in speech, in relationships, and in eating (as well as in many other areas). Being attentive to our thoughts and actions when it comes to why and how we eat is an area in which nepsis is a tangible tool, aiding us to care for soul *and* body.

As we continue through this book, we will learn how nepsis can apply to other areas of health. But for now, let's focus on the why and how of eating.

Some Questions to Consider

» Did you eat a bag of potato chips standing in the line at the post office? Why?

» Have you formed a habit of eating a snack at 2 PM (even

if it's a healthy one), even though you may not be hungry?

- Do you feel you are always leaving the table feeling uncomfortably stuffed?
- Is food something you feel you abuse in your life? Do you continually find yourself wanting to eat while doing other activities such as watching television, reading a book, or working on the computer?
- Do you tend to visit the break room at work on a regular basis, leaving with a cookie or a bag of pretzels?
- Do you pass by the kitchen and have a difficult time leaving without a snack in hand?
- Do you struggle with emotional or secret eating?
- Have desserts become breakfasts? Are foods falling out of their proper context as you constantly feed your sweet tooth throughout the day?

At this point, let's pause to reflect. Start to become attentive to your thoughts, feelings, and actions around eating. As we move through the upcoming chapters in this book, we will discuss additional strategies to handle these and many other areas. But we must have a reference point: we need to see where we are, and we need to recognize what sorts of eating behaviors we desire to change.

In order to turn away from these unwanted behaviors, we must have a plan of action in place, and we'll get to that in a bit.

Training Tool

At this point you may want to consider keeping a journal of your thoughts as we travel through the rest of this book together. A good old-fashioned pen and paper can do the trick. There are also areas in this book for you to jot down your thoughts. Or you may want to consider keeping an electronic journal or even starting a blog where others can read about your journey.

A blog may be a good idea as you will receive instant accountability and support. People will be waiting for your posts (accountability) and will likely comment on them (support). In addition, the blog may be a way for you to lend a helping hand to others in need of bettering their health.

SECTION 2

An Unhealthy Obsession with Healthy Eating

Those who have an unhealthy obsession with otherwise healthy eating may be suffering from *orthorexia nervosa,* a term that literally means "fixation on righteous eating." This term was coined by Dr. Steven Bratman, and it seems worth mentioning because this can be an unhealthy habit to develop. We've all heard the expression, "Too much of a good thing can actually be bad."

Many times when I meet new people, I find myself with one secret wish: I don't want the new people to know I'm a dietitian, because I feel if they find out, then for the rest of our time together, nutrition topics will dominate the conversation.

And the conversation will inevitably drift to a diet fad that is in the news, or one that is discussed in magazines, or one being pushed aggressively by a television celebrity, or one that is making the rounds on the internet. It's tough: we're living in a world where we're constantly being bombarded by, even sold, all sorts of outlandish dietary schemes.

The simple act of eating has become one of the most confusing daily tasks on the planet. Egg yolks, yikes; carbs—even worse. The point here is many of us are becoming so obsessed with healthy eating that it's taking on the role of an idol in our life.

Overly obsessing about healthy eating is moving us away from allowing our relationship with food to be a time to care for body and soul—an act of communing with God. Obsessing about healthy eating may also slowly open the door to prideful eating and lifestyle, leading us to the act of wrongfully judging the way others are eating and living.

In this context, it might be wise to take note of the wisdom shared by Saint Seraphim of Sarov: "Sitting at meals, do not look and do not judge how much any eats, but be attentive to yourself, nourishing your soul with prayer."

If this describes any of us—if we feel health and eating have become slightly unhealthy obsessions—it is good for us now to pause and take note. Yes, living and eating healthfully are important, but we must make sure we're not losing sight of the most important focus: making certain all our efforts are rooted in a spiritual context.

In the words of Saint Mark the Ascetic (fifth century), "Do not think about or do anything without a spiritual purpose, whereby it is done for God. For if you travel without purpose, you shall labor in vain."

Let's Keep the Right Spirit

Our actions—whether eating, exercising, drawing, or working—need to be acts that glorify God. In 1 Corinthians 10:31, Saint Paul reminds us, "Therefore, whether you eat or drink, or whatever you do, do all to the glory of God." We need to keep the right spirit when we're choosing to do things, including caring for our health. We shouldn't care for our health simply in order to look (or even to feel) better.

Rather, we should see caring for our health as an opportunity, a discipline, a path that leads to communing with the Divine. A happy by-product of this could well be losing sixteen pounds, or reducing gastric reflux, or normalizing blood sugar and blood pressure, and so forth.

At mealtime, let's practice some actions that, God willing, may lead us to cultivating eating as a sacred act. Let's start by reflecting and giving attention to the reasons we eat. When do we eat? Where do we eat? Why do we eat? These questions will be extremely important as we move forward into the upcoming areas of healthy behavior changes—as we continually strive to practice nepsis.

Training Tool

In the box below, document one or two areas of your eating patterns that you feel you need to improve. Examples:

» Snack way too often
» Consume too many sweet foods and drinks
» Eat portions of food that are way too large
» Eat when feeling emotionally down
» Obsess about healthy eating and lifestyle

SECTION 3

Prayer as a Way to Honor Mealtime

Saint Basil the Great, an early Church Father, teaches us to do the following:

> When you sit down to eat, pray. When you eat bread, do so thanking Him for being so generous to you. If you drink wine, be mindful of Him who has given it to you for your pleasure and as a relief in sickness. When you dress, thank Him for His kindness in providing you with clothes. When you look at the sky and the beauty of the stars, throw yourself at God's feet and adore Him who in His wisdom has arranged things in this way. Similarly, when the sun goes down and when it rises, when you are asleep or awake, give thanks to God, who created and arranged all things for your benefit, to have you know, love, and praise their Creator.

Let's start by first remembering to say our prayers, before and after the meal. Many of us are faithful in starting our meal with a prayer, especially when we are in the company of others who pray. But many of us do not even realize that the after-meal prayer is one that has been passed down and practiced by saints, priests, monastics, and lay people for centuries before us.

> **Before Mealtime Prayer:** Begin with the Lord's Prayer and follow that with this short prayer: "O Christ God, bless the food and drink of Your servants, for You are holy, now and ever and unto ages of ages. Amen."
>
> **After Mealtime Prayer:** Here is one to consider using: "We thank You, O God, giver of all good things, for these gifts and for all Your mercies, and we bless Your holy name, always, now and ever and unto ages of ages. Amen."

Now you may be thinking, "I'm going to remember to say my before- and after-meal prayers every day." Permit me to say, I've said the same thing, and I'm always shocked at how many times I forget to say my *after-meal* prayer.

Even now, when I am partaking of a meal with friends or relatives who don't pray, they at least pause with me, as they know my typical routine before taking the first bite. Actually, what I find quite beautiful is that some friends have mentioned to me that they've continued to do this before their first bite—that is, pause—as they have come to recognize the meal as the blessing that it is.

It's that after-meal prayer that seems to get me. My belly is satisfied, and I'm content, so prayer seems to fall right out the window (reminding me of Eutychus in the Book of Acts). What has helped me make the after-meal prayer a practice I do more often than not is to say the prayer as soon as I remember that I forgot to say it. If I finish dinner at 7:30 PM, and then 10:00 PM rolls around and I'm watching a great movie and I remember I forgot to say my after-meal prayer, I say it right then.

Mealtime is a special time, and cultures have cherished this for centuries. Look specifically at certain cultures, and before the first bite is taken, you hear "*bon appétit*," "cheers," "enjoy," or something along these lines. This is a time that we should honor, celebrate, and appreciate.

Practicing our before- and after-mealtime prayers carves out a time of the day in which the act of eating becomes an opportunity to focus on and glorify God. The prayers allow us to practice gratefulness (which is a form of love) and aid us in practicing self-control while partaking of the food before us. They help us to recognize that when we eat, we are indeed communing with the Divine.

Let's return to honoring mealtime by creating awareness and mindfulness around the act of eating.

Training Tool

» Focus on making sure to say prayers before and after meals.
» Take a notecard and copy the before-meal prayer on one side and the after-meal prayer on the other.
» You may wish to enter the prayers into your smart phone.
» Do something to keep the prayers close to where you eat your meals. Then read them before and after mealtimes.

Before long, you'll have the prayers memorized and will be able to say them with a prayerful heart without the use of the notecard.

SECTION 4

Set Up Your Eating Space

There is much to be said in regard to beauty and eating. We can start with organization and décor.

A study conducted by neuroscientists at Princeton University showed that physical clutter in our surroundings competes for our attention, resulting in decreased performance and increased stress.[4] Professional organizers also report that people tend to feel overwhelmed, energy-drained, and unproductive as a result of clutter in their surrounding areas.

Whether we like it or not, clutter, like ants, infiltrates many of our eating areas. The eating table contains bills, the kids' homework, documents that need to be filed, cleaning products, and a pile of folded clothes. If we're going to cultivate eating as a sacred act, we need to set up our eating space and make it as clutter-free and organized as possible.

> *In all of our deeds God looks at the intention, whether we do it for His sake, or for the sake of some other intention.*
>
> —St. Maximos the Confessor

Think about the last

extraordinary dining experience you had. What was present to create beauty? Was the table adorned with a table runner, tablecloth, some flowers, and/or a lit candle? Eating time is a special time, and so, as much as we can, let's get creative in bringing beauty to our mealtime space.

The same holds true if you regularly have to eat meals away from home at a location such as work. Once, I had a job in which eating in my cubicle was the only option. It was not ideal, but I tried as much as possible to make lunchtime a sacred and mindful time.

I kept a green placemat and a multicolored cloth napkin in my desk drawer. When I was preparing to partake of my lunch, I would shove the keyboard aside; clear the desk of papers, pens, and everything else that somehow grew legs and walked onto my desk; and then set out my placemat. (Actually, I wanted to light a candle, too, but that went against company policy, so I decided to keep the job and forgo the mealtime mood lighting.) This simple act helped to signify that this time was indeed a special time.

I urge you to focus on doing this in your home and, if appropriate, in other environments where you regularly eat. Create your main mealtime space. Do something to create beauty in this area. As Dostoevsky said, "Beauty will save the world," and it may help us save our healthy-eating habits too.

Training Tool

What could you consider doing in your main mealtime space to make it a more sacred space? Here are some suggestions:

» Clear the table of clutter.
» Light a mealtime candle.
» Adorn the table with fresh flowers.
» Use a tablecloth or table runner.
» Hang an icon in your dining area—"Jesus Feeding the 5,000," "The Wedding at Cana," "The Last Supper," "The Hospitality of Abraham," and "Saint Samson the Patron Saint of Hospitality" are a few suggestions.
» Use cloth napkins. (Not only is this a way to beautify mealtime, it's also a small way for you to be a good steward of the earth.)
» Choose plates and cups that you feel are beautiful. (It's a form of functional art.) This does not have to be an expensive endeavor; some of my favorite plates I found at a local Goodwill store.

In the box below, indicate what you would like to do to beautify your main mealtime area:

SECTION 5

Start to Manage Mindless Munching

Sacred eating and mindless eating do not go hand in hand. Sitting down while eating is yet another way that helps us in making eating time a sacred time.

We should always try to sit down at a table when eating. Mindless eating happens much more easily when standing near counters, in front of refrigerators, or in the workplace hallway; it also happens when we're walking around downtown or in the mall, when we're in the car or bus, or when we're on the couch in front of the television.

Yet when we sit down at a mealtime table to eat, we bring attention to what we are about to do.

Training Tool

> Start by making the munch area a no-eating zone. Make yourself return to eating at the meal table.
>
> Sit down at a mealtime table (or at least try to pause and sit somewhere) when eating something; do this as much as possible.
>
> If you catch yourself standing and eating, take note of why it happened. The more we become aware and give mindful attention to our actions, the more we are likely to change our behavior.
>
> We need to learn from our actions, as they do have a lot to teach us. It might be worth keeping a journal

about some of your thoughts and actions in this area.

In the box below, name a place you tend to mindlessly munch. Indicate why you think it happens.

SECTION 6

Fill Your "Health Toolbox"

Now we start filling our "health toolbox." These tools will be needed to build our new foundation.

This book outlines a plan of action to turn away from the faulty floor plan that we were following in the past, and it allows us to create a new framework, a new outlook, a new way of thinking about our remodeled healthy house.

Let's put on our hardhats and get ready to do the work—turning away from the old and embracing the new. We want to build on a new solid foundation, and in so doing become joyful participants, ready and willing to do this necessary work. And we want to be pleased with our work because it will be done for the right reasons.

We want to change our eating habits—making eating into a sacred occasion—for a whole new reason: to deepen our communion with our Creator. (And by the way, other goals, such as fitting into our old jeans and lowering our blood pressure, might just happen.)

Training Tool

Think of what you personally need to do with your health to make sure you are caring for both body and soul. For example: Is your diabetes unmanaged? Have you put on extra weight? Are your triglycerides elevated?

In the box on the next page, document one major goal you would like to accomplish when it comes to your health. As we continue to move through this book together, we will be working on smaller goals to help us accomplish the larger goal. (Examples: Manage diabetes, bring down triglyceride levels, lose weight, handle the unhealthy obsession with food.)

If you're reading this book in a group, discuss how things are going. What were your struggles? What is working? Let someone else in the group know specific areas you are trying to work on in regard to your health.

If you're reading alone, you may want to consider keeping a journal (electronically or in the good old-fashioned pen-and-paper way). Or consider blogging about your week.

So far, we've looked at some of the teachings of the Orthodox Tradition, and we've suggested how they inform our thinking, especially when it comes to viewing eating as a sacred act.

Next, we'll focus on what we should—and should not—be eating.

CHAPTER TWO

Nourishing Our Body to Care for Our Soul

During the tenth century, the venerable Saint Simeon the New Theologian wrote, "Fasting is the mother of health; the friend of chastity; the partner of humble-mindedness (illnesses are frequently born in many from a disorderly and irregular diet)."

In the tenth century, Saint Simeon was taking note of what we're trying to prove scientifically in the twenty-first. I'm amazed by some of the research studies being conducted these days. Do we really need to spend millions of dollars on a study to tell us that drinking too much soda can be a cause of weight problems and diabetes?

We must eat. It's a fact: Eating gives us our physical strength and energy to perform our daily physical and spiritual work.

Saint Seraphim of Sarov teaches, "Every day one should partake of just enough food to permit the body, being fortified, to be a friend and helper to the soul in performing the virtues. Otherwise, with the body exhausted, the soul may also weaken." In light of this wisdom, we need to eat foods that fortify our bodies. *Fortify* is a key word.

To put it another way, we need to eat foods that nourish us—and provide our body with the nutrients it needs. Foods that nourish are rarely the cause of a diet that leads to illness. But not all so-called "foods" are nourishing, leading us to ask the question: What is in our foods that we need to be aware of?

SECTION 1

A Look at "Food"

Eating was much easier 150 years ago when foods came primarily from farms, ranches, oceans, and rivers. However, now we're dealing with what many refer to as "fake foods."

Many food products on the market today are marketed as "healthy," but in reality, they are wreaking havoc with our health. Something as basic as our food system is now in a conundrum. Numerous "health" foods have been produced that contain harmful additives, and artificial foods are taking the place of natural ones.

In fact, many fake foods currently on the market were created with good intentions. Take margarine, for example:

> *As for butter versus margarine, I trust cows more than chemists.*
> —Joan Dye Gussow

During the Great Depression when butter became really expensive, the inventor of margarine thought he was helping out with the situation by creating something he felt resembled butter. Into a laboratory he went, and presto! Margarine (partially hydrogenated oil, a synthetic trans fat) was born. His selling point was that it could be produced for a much cheaper price than that of butter.

Long after the Great Depression, modern-day scientists and health experts conveyed to the public that margarine was the healthier alternative. We received the message that it was better for our heart, for diabetes management, and for health in general. Yet now the experts are saying, "Oops, we made a mistake . . . butter is better."

High-fructose corn syrup is another example. This man-designed sweetener was introduced in greater amounts into our food system during the years 1975 to 1985. Again, the inventor of high-fructose corn syrup thought the product would help feed the masses for a low price. Now we see high-fructose corn syrup as a potential factor leading to conditions such as diabetes, heart disease, obesity, and cancer.

Many of the world's largest artificial-flavor production companies design artificial flavors in drinks to make us want to come back for more. They actually design drink flavorings

> *We are living in a world today where lemonade is made from artificial flavors and furniture polish is made from real lemons.*
> —Alfred E. Neuman

that create a burst of flavor in our mouths and then suddenly die off, urging us to take another sip and yet another. Shocking, right? It's almost as if they were in the business of creating food and beverage addictions. If that's not alarming enough, believe it or not, a single artificial flavoring is made up of a combination of hundreds of individual non-food-based chemicals.

Petroleum-based artificial food dyes (yes, *petroleum*, the stuff that makes our cars go *vroom, vroom*) have such a strong and convincing link with hyperactivity disorder in children that throughout Europe (starting around 2008) artificial food dyes have been banned from use in foods.[5]

On a positive note, several food industry companies are voluntarily choosing to dye foods with basic (natural) ingredients found in God's creation, using such items as spices and vegetables—turmeric and beets being examples.

Saint Paisios, a twentieth-century saint, states, "Today people make illicit and deceitful businesses. However, they should not falsify food substances, because they become the cause of harming people's health."[6]

The evil one never sleeps. Personally, I think he works overtime when throwing his crafty darts at our food system.

The margarine and high-fructose corn syrup inventors thought they were helping us out; they had what probably appeared to them to be good and noble intentions.

But now we know that our bodies do not like this artificial stuff, and our bodies need to be *fortified* with real food. Our bodies are screaming, "Please don't gulp down another high-fructose-corn-syrup-laden beverage." They're saying, "Please, no more artificial food dyes." They are saying, "Feed me and feed me foods that fortify me." They're not trying to be complainers. They're simply asking us to feed them what their Creator intended them to be fed.

As already noted, we must struggle, and the more we know, the better tools and strategies we have in place to deal with the struggle. Many of these food additives currently present in our foods weren't even in existence three hundred years ago. Some of these modern-day preservatives and additives can be harmful to our health and increase our food cravings. We must make the commitment to limit—or better, to stop—partaking of the foods that we know contain them.

> *Food is an important part of a balanced diet.*
>
> —Fran Lebowitz

Training Tool

Take a look in your kitchen and scrutinize the food labels of prepackaged food products you consume.

Note the labels that contain any of the following:

- High-fructose corn syrup
- Partially hydrogenated oils (examples: partially hydrogenated soybean oil, partially hydrogenated cotton seed oil)
- Artificial flavorings
- Artificial food dyes (examples: Blue 1, Blue 2, Citrus Red 2, Green 3, Orange B, Red 3, Red 40, Yellow 5, Yellow 6)

Here are some examples of fake foods and drinks to remove: Gatorade, Coke, Country Crock Original Vegetable Oil Spread, Skittles, etc.

Now, in the box below, list three foods and/or drinks you consume on a fairly regular basis that contain any of the ingredients we have mentioned:

SECTION 2

Eat from the Earth

If we are to change our eating habits and dependence on fake foods, what should we do? Do we have to settle for a diet that is made up of bland rice cakes and unsalted boiled cabbage? Must we forgo desserts and eat only fruits and vegetables? To put it simply: The answer is NO!

> *He causes the grass to grow*
> *for the cattle,*
> *And vegetation for the*
> *service of man,*
> *That he may bring forth*
> *food from the earth,*
> *And wine that makes glad*
> *the heart of man,*
> *Oil to make his face shine,*
> *And bread which strengthens*
> *man's heart.*
>
> PSALM 104(105):14–15

What we need to do is start by eating primarily from God's creation (earthly ingredients). If the food didn't exist during the time of the apostles, then we probably shouldn't be eating it. Okay, this might be an exaggeration, but a fun one to keep in the back of our minds—as I'm sure the apostles weren't enjoying quiche Lorraine for brunch. Yet quiche is a fine food to enjoy, because all the ingredients that go into it were around when the apostles were living: eggs, butter, flour, cream, cheese, veggies, etc. All they were missing was a hardback edition of *The Joy of Cooking* cookbook.

Let's start by eating primary ingredients from God's creation: fruits, vegetables, meats, eggs, fish, beans, nuts, milk, honey, grains, rice, etc.—and all foods made from these primary ingredients, such as cheese, bread, butter, noodles, olive oil, and so forth.

Here are some basic guidelines to follow: If it grew out of the ground or on a tree, eat it. If it was derived from an

> *You can do a lot for your diet by eliminating foods that have mascots.*
> —TED SPIKER

animal, eat it. If it was synthetically produced by people wearing white lab coats instead of kitchen aprons, don't eat it!

God made cows, and from them we get milk, and from milk we get butter and cream. God did not make I-Can't-Believe-It's-Not Butter or Coffee-mate creamer. He made the real deal (real food).

God made sugarcane, and He created bees that make honey, trees that produce maple syrup, and bushes that yield the herb stevia. God did not make high-fructose corn syrup, aspartame (NutraSweet), saccharin (Sweet 'n' Low), or sucralose (Splenda).

God made primary ingredients, and we should relish the art of combining them and tasting them together. Noodles, cheese, meat, tomatoes: lasagna, anyone? Broccoli, rice, carrots: stir-fry, anyone?

Let's start by eating food from God's creation. Now take a moment and locate one of your thumbs. This thumb goes everywhere you go, right? This thumb is going to be your new healthy-shopping buddy.

Whenever you're buying any prepackaged food, use this rule of thumb: If the list of ingredients is longer than your thumb, and if you can't pronounce half the things on the list, and if you have no clue what the majority of the ingredients are, then you probably shouldn't be eating them.

Become a food-ingredient-label detective. Remove foods from your diet that contain fake ingredients, and replace these foods with real foods.

Training Tool

Here is a starter list of fake ingredients that we want to try to avoid as much as possible. This will be your guide. Type this list into your smart phone or write it on an index card that will go to the grocery store with you (along with your thumb).

Try to limit or avoid foods that contain these ingredients:

- » Partially hydrogenated oil of any kind (for example, partially hydrogenated soybean oil or partially hydrogenated cottonseed oil)
- » Artificial sweeteners, including aspartame, sucralose, saccharin, acesulfame-K
- » High-fructose corn syrup
- » Food dyes (examples: Red Dye 40, Blue 2, Yellow lake 5, etc.)
- » Sodium nitrite
- » Sodium nitrate
- » Monosodium glutamate
- » BHT (This is how it will appear on the food label.)
- » BHA (This is how it will appear on the food label.)
- » Potassium bromate
- » Propyl gallate
- » Brominated Vegetable Oil (BVO)
- » TBHQ (This is how it will appear on the food label.)

The Center for Science in the Public Interest does extensive research on many ingredients found in our foods that are harmful to health and could possibly be sabotaging our weight-loss efforts. If you're interested in more information on preservatives and additives that should be removed from your diet, check out their website; it is an invaluable resource (http://cspinet.org/reports/chemcuisine.htm).

Let's simplify this eating circus we're all wrapped up in. When we eat foods that God gave us and designed us to have a relationship with, we will be giving ourselves foods that our bodies know how to process. But when we eat fake foods that are loaded with synthetics and artificial ingredients, our bodies will be taxed when they attempt to process them.

By cleaning up our diets and focusing on eating real foods, we optimize the functioning of our bodies. This aids our health in many areas, including lowering chronic-disease risks, controlling weight, and improving energy levels.

SECTION 3

The Basics of a Balanced Diet

Related to choosing real foods to eat, we must remember this: Choosing real foods does not mean our eating can become a free-for-all. We all know these diet fads, right? "Eat all the protein you want, but don't you dare think of even sniffing a carb." "Eat all the low-fat foods you want, but don't even consider touching a coconut, an avocado, or a pat of butter."

It's important that we have balance in our diets. Current research emphasizes that a diet rich in fruits and vegetables is a good base for a balanced, healthy, and nutritious diet. We need to ensure that these foods are the primary building blocks of our diet.

Many fruits and vegetables go above and beyond what they're expected to do to sustain our lives. They outshine many foods because they also contain beneficial bonuses such as antioxidants (molecules that may block the effects of harmful chemicals known as free radicals, aiding in the prevention of diseases) and flavonoids (plant-based pigments in foods that may also provide health benefits to the body).

The components of fruits and vegetables have been shown to help in the prevention and management of cancers and other chronic diseases. They're kind of the "showoffs" when it comes to foods. They give us what we need—vitamin C and vitamin A, along with a plethora of other necessary nutrients—and they throw in these super plant-based components (antioxidants and flavonoids) to take care of our health even more.

Let's Talk about Sweeteners

Dessert: Isn't that one of the main reasons we eat dinner? The World Health Organization (WHO) recently released a statement that humans should consume no more than six teaspoons of added sugar a day.[7]

Now it is imperative to note that *added* sugar does not include the sugars naturally found in fresh produce, such as an apple or a sweet potato. Nor does it apply to the sugar naturally found in dairy products, such as milk and plain yogurt. The added sugars include many sweeteners used in manufactured foods such as cereals, lemonade, ketchup, flavored yogurts, granola bars, and so forth.

It would be helpful if added sugars were required to be listed in grams per serving on our food labels. But this is not currently the case, though change may be coming. This would make it easy to know how much added sugar per serving we are actually eating when consuming a prepackaged product.

Other sources of added sugar we consume include honey, table sugar, maple syrup, fruit concentrates, and so forth. Some examples would be the teaspoon of honey we put in our morning cup of tea; or that teaspoon and a half of sugar that is baked into the homemade brownie we are enjoying for dessert.

Six teaspoons per day! When I read this suggested amount given by the WHO, I thought, "Gosh, that's quite generous." In Appendix III are some charts that demonstrate how easy it is to stay under that amount per day, and how easy it is to go over it.

A can of soda is one of the easiest ways to exceed the maximum daily amount of sugar. On average, there are close to ten teaspoons of sweetener in one twelve-ounce can; and usually that sweetener is in the form of high-fructose corn syrup, one of the fake sweeteners we want to avoid.

Let's look at a study that helps illustrate why we want to run from high-fructose corn syrup. Researchers demonstrated that not all sweeteners are the same. They looked specifically at high-fructose corn syrup—a major sweetener found in so many of America's fruit drinks, sodas, ketchups, yogurts, cereals, and breads.

Carla set up a nutrition-counseling session because her doctor told her she was pre-diabetic and her liver enzymes were elevated. The first thing she did was cut out all foods that contained high-fructose corn syrup. This step alone was enough to bring blood sugar levels and liver enzymes back into normal range. Carla continued to make other changes to her diet and is no longer considered pre-diabetic.

Some rats were given high-fructose corn syrup, and other rats were given sugar. Even when the number of calories the two groups were consuming was the same, the high-fructose-corn-syrup-fed rats gained more weight and had a greater increase in triglycerides (a type of fat circulating in the blood that when elevated can put a person at risk for heart disease).

In addition, the researchers observed more fat being deposited in the abdominal region; and research indicates when weight gain occurs in this region and triglyceride levels are elevated, a person could be at risk for diabetes, cancer, and coronary artery disease.[8]

What does this mean for us? This means that when we do choose to consume foods that contain sweetener, we first and foremost want to make sure they contain sweeteners God made.

Moreover, we also want to place sugar in its proper context. (We'll talk about this in more detail in sections to come.) Right now, it is enough to note that on average Americans are eating close to sixty pounds of sweetener per year. Yes, you read that correctly: sixty pounds.[9]

That amount is equivalent to approximately 6,800 teaspoons of sugar per year—about 19 teaspoons per day. This far exceeds the WHO's recommendation of no more than 6 teaspoons per day (or 2,100 teaspoons per year). And, of course, the more we can stay under this recommended amount, the better!

So what do we do? Do we hop on a completely sugar-free, cardboard-tasting, lack-of-enjoyment dietary regimen? I trust you will answer, NO! Where we should start is to place foods and drinks back into their proper context.

Think about soda parlors. These establishments started to

develop around 1903. A guy would find a nice date, get all dressed up, slick his hair to one side, and off to the soda parlor they'd go.

Both people would enjoy a soda that was made with sugar—and mind you, it wasn't the Double Big Gulp 64-ounce cup that you need an octopus's assistance to get a sip out of. Rather, it was a normal-sized cup. In fact, in the 1950s, the average soda size was 7 ounces. Now we can get a bottled soda that is at least 20 ounces. Moreover, you can go to a restaurant and order a 42-ounce soda—and more than likely it comes with a free refill!

That occasional romantic trip to the soda parlor, to see and flirt with the soda jerk and to have a soda, was exactly that—an occasion. What we are seeing now is that soda (be it diet or regular) has become a standard drink to have with our lunches and at our office desks as we work away.

Yes, we may still consume sweeteners, but the amounts and the types we choose are key. Right now, let's focus on placing food and drink back into their proper context. We recognize that we do need to keep our sweetener intake under control, and we do need to choose the real versions. (Please

A great friend of mine, Nick, was drinking 40 to 60 ounces of soda daily. We made a pact he would not have soda for a month. By day 23 he had lost 19 pounds and his blood pressure normalized.

check out Appendices II and III for some replacements for both diet and regular sodas.)

We also want to eat foods, as much as possible, that are coming from God's creation. All this ties into saying "no" to artificial sweeteners.

Artificial sweeteners such as saccharin (Sweet 'n' Low), sucralose (Splenda), and aspartame (Nutrasweet, Equal) have had countless studies conducted on their effects on the human body. Evidence suggests that frequent consumption may cause excessive weight gain, type 2 diabetes, cardiovascular disease, and metabolic syndrome. (Metabolic syndrome includes increased blood pressure, high blood-sugar level, excess body fat around the waist, and abnormal cholesterol levels.)[10]

Examples of Natural Sweeteners God Made	Examples of Altered and Artificial Sweeteners Man Made
Sugarcane	High-fructose corn syrup
Honey	Aspartame
Maple syrup	Artificial maple syrup
Stevia	Sucralose

Now we can ask: What's the wisdom in all this? Simply put, we need to eat the real deal and do so in a sensible amount (we'll get to "sensible amounts" in the chapter to come). Even when I work with diabetics, I do not recommend artificial sweeteners; we work together to incorporate real sweeteners into their dietary patterns, and if the diabetic is severely sugar-intolerant, we use the all-natural, calorie-free herb stevia. Yet again, even for diabetics, avoiding the artificial ingredients and using less of the real deal is the better option.

Training Tool

In the box below, indicate the main form of sweetener you are currently using. If you are currently using a fake sweetener on a regular basis, what would you consider doing to rid your diet of this fake substance? Example: "I am currently using the sweetener Splenda in my coffee. I will switch to using Sugar In the Raw in my coffee."

SECTION 4

Let's Talk about Fat

This is actually a perfect time to talk about fat, because the fat and sugar scenarios go hand-in-hand. We'll see why this is the case in a few moments, but for now, let's take a peek in my mom's delicious kitchen.

I grew up putting full-fat plain yogurt on my rice. No

fat-free or low-fat versions allowed in my mom's fridge. Then when I started to study nutrition, I began to get confused. I kept hearing "low-fat this," "fat-free that," so I decided to try to gently persuade my mom in this direction. "Mom," I said, "this is what they're teaching us to tell our patients with whom we do nutrition counseling" (even though I myself didn't think it tasted remotely natural, or good for that matter).

My mom looked at me with puzzlement in her beautiful green eyes. She was probably thinking, "Why am I paying so much for her to get this education?"

In her firm yet loving voice, she said, "Rita, this is the way people have been eating yogurt for centuries—unadulterated, fat and all. It seems to me God wants the fat in there, so we shouldn't take it out. Why don't you tell people to stick to eating the full-fat version and just eat less of it?"

That response led me to question why I was even pursuing this education in nutrition. If I just told people to consume foods the way my mom had prepared them for me from my childhood, I could have saved us all a lot of tuition and room-and-board money.

Nevertheless, I continued with my schooling, learning a lot as well as recognizing the importance of looking back—looking back at how my mom fed us; at how our ancestors ate; at how certain cultures ate, cultures that were and are still healthy today.

I have the blessing of working for the company Mediterranean Wellness, and this is exactly what we do. We use the Mediterranean people—those who still hold to their traditional eating patterns—as an example for modern-day healthy eating guidelines.

As much as my brothers and I thought it would have been better to have the boxes of brightly colored cereal, TV dinners, SpaghettiOs, and powdered pudding boxes in our home, these items were never there.

We ate olives; we ate eggs; we ate hummus; we ate rice; we ate chicken; we ate yogurt; we ate salads; we ate ice cream. Furthermore, as a special treat, my dad would make his "family-famous" homemade potato chips. I can still picture him cutting those potatoes as thin as he possibly could, then lightly frying them in olive oil.

I can't continue without mentioning the many pomegranates he opened for us. I've lost count of the nice shirts he stained during the process. Giving us this treat as soon as possible was more important than changing out of his work shirt—even though my mom pleaded with him to put on an old shirt or apron as she foresaw the tie-dyed design that would result from his pomegranate-dissecting endeavor.

When my mom moved to this country, she did not change her traditional ways of eating, even though she was being told to use margarine instead of butter and fat-free yogurt instead of plain old full-fat yogurt.

Let us attend to the way our ancestors ate. Let us look at foods from the past. Let us eat like the apostles; hence, when choosing foods, don't be misled toward choosing the low-fat or fat-free versions.

Dr. Paul Rozin from the University of Pennsylvania, a researcher who has conducted countless studies about eating practices in America, notes that a substantial minority of Americans hold the belief that fat is a toxin.[11] A macronutrient that is essential for life has been labeled as a toxin in our society. Yikes!

After attending a "Food, Faith, and Fasting" workshop and reading several newspaper articles about the dangers of trans fats, Robert finally connected the dots when for the first time he read the ingredient label for Coffee-mate dairy creamer and realized that it was essentially trans fat. He stopped putting Coffee-mate in his cup of coffee.

We've made quite a few wrong turns when it comes to eating our traditional foods. Here, for example, are the ingredients that make up Coffee-mate, copied directly from a label: "Corn syrup solids, vegetable oil (partially hydrogenated coconut or palm kernel, hydrogenated soybean), sugar, sodium caseinate (a milk derivative), dipotassium phosphate, and less than 2% of color added, mono- and diglycerides, sodium aluminosilicate, artificial and natural flavors, salt, annatto color."

Does that sound like something we eagerly want to add to our freshly brewed morning cup of joe? If the apostles were going to sip a cup of coffee, is that what they would be putting in it?

Now let's take a look at half-and-half. The ingredients are listed as "cream and milk." Cream and milk, pretty basic, and it seems as if that's what our ancestors would've put in their coffee.

Remember what we discussed about the evil one being so deceitful and working tricks with our food system? Check this out: Tablespoon by tablespoon, half-and-half has fewer calories per serving (17.5) than Coffee-mate powdered non-fat dairy creamer (30). Yes, you read correctly: the non-fat dairy creamer has almost twice the calories of the full-fat half-and-half. We see the words "fat-free" dancing across the front of the Coffee-mate container, and we assume it's the better choice.

To return to eating the way our ancestors ate: as mentioned above, we must read the ingredients on our prepackaged foods. The front of the box is where fabulous claims are made and pictures of famous people are placed. The ingredient list is where the company has to 'fess up and be honest.

Now, let's go back to our friend Fat. He's not the bad guy; in fact, fat is our friend.

Small amounts of real fat (not the fake, partially hydrogenated, synthetically created concoction) in the diet can help keep us satisfied between meals, which helps us cut down on between-meal snacking. This is because, to simplify, fat is processed very slowly in the body, keeping us satisfied for a longer period of time.

Not that we're working toward counting calories here, but let's look at an example to illustrate: If we add, let's say, 40 calories in the form of a fat to our breakfast—maybe through a drizzle of cream on our oatmeal, or some walnuts could do the trick—this could help to prevent a 200-calorie midmorning snack. As a result, at the end of the day, who is eating fewer calories: the person who's eating fat-free versions or the person who's having a moderate amount of fat at meals?

Because so many of us are running away from fat, we end up wanting to snack all day long. We're not cows. Cows can get away with grazing all day long as they were created to eat grass. I'm quite sure if God had created us to eat only grass, we would need to graze all day long too.

However, God created us to eat, then work, and eat again, then work, and finally eat again. We've moved away from the three-meals-a-day concept. Today, let's start by trying as much as possible to go back to three meals a day versus the six to eight small meals/snacks we may be currently having. Now, of course, if a person has to eat six meals as a way to manage a medical condition, that's fine, but as much as possible, let's return to eating at meal times and move away from munching all day long.

This takes us back to chapter one in regard to honoring eating time, making it a sacred time. It is easier to munch when we allow eating to happen anywhere and everywhere: in the car, at the desk, in front of the TV, on the bus, at the meeting. However, when we return to regular meals, a lot of excess-munching opportunities come to a halt.

Why do we feel satisfied when we're eating moderate amounts of fat? It all has to do with how fat is processed in the body. It is processed very slowly, giving us a sustained amount of energy over a longer period of time. That is why moderate amounts of fat incorporated into a diabetic's meal plan can help in blood-sugar control. Fat has been shown time and time again to help in stabilizing a diabetic's blood sugar.[12]

Now again, we're not talking about the free-for-all, all-you-can-eat-fat diet here; in fact, we won't ever talk about the all-you-can-eat approach in this book. We are talking about placing foods in their proper context.

We are recognizing that a little bit of fat can go a long way. Remember, fat is our friend. Fat isn't bad; it's what we do with the fats that can make them bad. If we eat too much fat, or if we eat the synthetic, partially hydrogenated oil fats (trans fats), well then, fat is bad.

But when fat is just a part of an overall healthful diet and is incorporated sensibly into meal times, that's a healthy thing to do. This is an age-old way people have been eating since long before high triglycerides and elevated cholesterol were a concern.

Let's try to overcome some of the snares the evil one has set for us, such as fake ingredients sabotaging our foods and the beneficial ingredients being removed from them. Let's get rid of the fat-free mentality, and in the spirit of Dr. Seuss, let's remember this playful rhyme:

> If the Creator made it,
> It's okay if we ate it.

And, of course, we must be mindful of portion size, the subject of the next chapter.

Training Tool

In the box on the next page, indicate a food that in its unadulterated form would contain fat, but you consume the low-fat or fat-free version. What would you be willing to try to do in order to move toward the unmodified version of the food?

Examples:

» Yogurt. I usually consume low-fat yogurt with fruit on the bottom; I would consider trying a smaller portion of the full-fat plain version and adding my own fixings (use the sample recipes found in Appendix II).

» I usually consume fat-free milk. I would consider using the whole-milk version and using less of it.

SECTION 5

Brown vs. White

We always want to move away from processed foods as much as possible. White rice vs. brown rice? Both are fine; brown rice is just richer in nutrients. At least white rice has not been chemically created and altered. It's just missing something that's good.

But what it's missing are nutrients we can get from other foods. Some of these nutrients are iron, B vitamins, and fiber. Complementing white rice with a side of veggies is a great way to attain these nutrients; in addition, it will aid us in controlling the amount of rice we consume.

Just like fat, carbohydrates (carbs) are not bad; it's what we do with them that can make them bad. Choosing highly processed, sweetener-laden carbs is not the best choice. Having portion-controlled amounts of the real deal (real food) is a fine and tasty thing to do.

Brown breads vs. white breads: Again, brown breads do contain more B vitamins, vitamin E, and fiber, but these are nutrients we can also get from other foods. We could go ahead and have the white baguette, if we prefer, but we just need to make sure to eat it with some veggies and other foods that contain fat and/or protein, such as cheese or olive oil.

White flour, it's important to note, lacks fiber, so we want to make sure we have some fat and fiber foods in the meal when consuming white versions of bread products to help prevent a drastic rise in blood sugar.

The take-home message from all of this is: Whether we're choosing white or brown, it all comes down to portions consumed and combining the carbohydrate source (be it bread, pasta, or rice) with foods that offer fiber, protein, and fats.

The reality is our body does not need a ton of carbs, yet many of us are eating way more than our body's fair share. This excessive carb intake common in American culture is one of the reasons many are suffering from chronic inflammation, elevated triglycerides, diabetes, and excess weight.

Yes, our body needs carbs, but we need to eat them in balance and control. The control issue we will handle in the next chapter. Portion control is key to healthy eating, so stay tuned! For now, the menus in Appendix III (non-fasting and fasting options—fasting will be discussed in chapter four) will give us an idea of how to balance meals with carbohydrates, fats, and protein.

Again, brown is a good choice, but if you're having white—just have it right. To further exemplify this brown vs. white issue, look to the older, more established yummy food cultures of the world: Italy, France, and Japan.

In Italy, the Italians savor every bite of their white pasta topped with olive oil and Parmesan cheese, but we'll never find the all-you-can-eat bottomless bowl of pasta some Americanized Italian restaurants offer. Pasta is eaten in sensible portions.

I think a Frenchwoman would knock me over the head with her fresh, warm, white baguette if I tried to take it away from her; but again, in France, we'd never find the twelve-inch sub that many American fast-food joints offer.

Finally, imagine trying to tell a Japanese person there will be no white rice served with their *sashimi*. They'd probably look at us as people with three heads. But again, we would never see them being served two cups of rice as we see at our Americanized Japanese eateries.

Training Tool

In the box on the next page, write down your current personal observations on your carbohydrate intake. Do you think you eat more carbs than your body needs, or just the right amount?

For now, you just want to take note of where you are with this, as it will be vital when we move into the portion-control chapter. Taking this moment to pause and observe your current dietary practices should aid you to become a more mindful eater.

SECTION 6

Let's Return to the Joy of Eating

During one internet surfing session, I read this comment on an Eastern Orthodox blog, and it stuck with me. The head cook from the Lensa Monastery in France stated, "We always try to have a balanced, nutritious, and tasty meal, so that people do not waste their time dreaming about food or trying to eat out."

We're not going to take the joy out of eating. In fact, we're doing just the opposite: we are going to allow mealtime to be a time to commune with the Divine. We are going to return to eating delicious foods from our Creator's creation. However, we're going to eat them in control, and in so doing nourish our bodies with proper nutrients in the appropriate amounts.

Training Tool

In the box below, indicate two things you are willing to do that will add balance, nutrition, and taste to your meals. (Examples: Move away from using low-fat and fat-free products; move away from consuming artificial ingredients; move toward using real ingredients and enjoying them in control.)

Additional Training Tool

Check out these easy recipes provided in Appendix II to replace common foods that may contain fake ingredients.

- Salad dressing
- Yogurt for breakfast

- Macaroni and cheese
- Sausage patties
- Grape spritzers (this is a great replacement for diet and regular sodas)
- Ramen noodle soup
- Granola

  Choose a recipe or a prepackaged food you commonly prepare that contains fake ingredients, and alter and prepare it to contain only real food.

So far, we've looked at the call to practice sacred eating and at the urgency of eating real (and not fake) foods. Now we move to another crucial turn in our journey to better health through eating: portion control.

CHAPTER THREE

Eating Less for More Flavor

Now that we know real food satisfies, it makes sense that this would be the first step in portion control. Let's stick to eating foods that our Creator created. It's simply a nutritious (and delicious) place to start.

Father Alexander Schmemann, in his book *For the Life of the World,* states:

> When we see the world as an end in itself, everything becomes itself a value and consequently loses all value, because only in God is found the meaning (value) of everything, and the world is meaningful only when it is the "sacrament" of God's presence. Things treated merely as things in themselves destroy themselves because only in God have they any life. The world of nature, cut off from the source of life, is a dying world. For one who thinks food in itself is the source of life, eating is communion with the dying world, it

> is communion with death. Food itself is dead, it is life that has died and it must be kept in refrigerators like a corpse.[13]

SECTION 1

Eating as Communing with the Divine

When we approach eating as a time to commune with the Divine, eating goes deeper than simply taking bites for nourishment. In other words, we are doing something more than merely "feeding the machine." Eating takes on a new meaning: food becomes more than the gasoline (energy) for our cars (bodies).

When we wholeheartedly embrace eating with the mindset of it being an opportunity to commune with the Divine, the act of eating is transformed into something richer and far more meaningful than it once was in our mind. Eating becomes a time to use our senses through the act of partaking in a meal to be with God.

Embracing this approach to eating frames this daily activity in a different way. We take the focus off counting calories and grams of fiber, and we enjoy our meals—and things just happen: cholesterol comes under control, excess weight is lost, blood sugar stabilizes, elevated triglycerides decrease, gastric reflux subsides, chronic diseases are managed or prevented, and so forth.

The choice is ours. We can choose one of two ways to look at our relationship with food. We can see it simply as feeding the machine, or as a time to commune with God.

It is not necessarily the grams of this and the milligrams of the other that need to change; what needs to change is our relationship with food.

Training Tool

In the box below, briefly define what you currently feel your relationship with food looks like.

SECTION 2

Eat to Live, Don't Live to Eat

As we mentioned earlier, the venerable Saint Simeon the New Theologian, who lived in the tenth century, noted that "illnesses are frequently born in many from a disorderly and irregular diet." This can simply refer to eating too much.

Saint Simeon said this long ago, but it's so relevant for our current-day eating frenzy with the all-you-can-eat, Supersize everything, portions equating to the size of a pick-up truck.

In a book on the American celebrity Ellen Degeneres, the writer Kathleen Tracy quotes Ellen as saying, "We've got all-you-can-eat places. We don't need to be eating all we can eat! We're not bears; we're not hibernating!"[14] The way Ellen puts it is funny, but in reality it is true—and sad.

We're living in a day and age where bigger is better. On a mass level, our food culture has drastically changed. The National Institute of Health explains that twenty years ago, a standard bagel was three inches in diameter and contained 140 calories. Today bagels are close to six inches in diameter, containing 350 calories.

> *Nothing that God has created is in itself bad. Food is not bad, gluttony is; the procreation of children is not bad, lechery is; wealth is not bad, avarice is; glory is not bad, only vainglory is. So you see nothing is bad in itself, only the misuse of it, which is the soul's negligence in cultivating its true nature.*
>
> —St. Maximos the Confessor

We're currently eating more and sitting more. I'm sure we can agree this is *not* the best equation for health. I haven't heard one health expert who touts the benefits of eating more than our body needs or of being as sedentary as we can possibly be.

Back in the day when we were primarily eating from the farms, oceans, rivers, and gardens, we had to labor for our food. We were unable to pop something in the microwave and have a meal hot and ready in thirty seconds flat.

It was virtually impossible to instantly consume 250 calories, as we are able to do now by simply ripping open a bag of chips. In those early days, if people were going to eat potatoes, they would have to prepare the potatoes.

Our ancestors would burn calories simply through the act of kneading dough, fishing, and harvesting apples. In addition, desserts were not as accessible. We did not have the option of eating a cookie or cupcake simply by opening up the package. We had to put energy, time, and planning into creating these treats.

Things have changed. Prepared food, simply ready to eat at the watering of our mouths, is everywhere. This poses great challenges for us. We have to be even more on guard to ensure that we are eating mindfully. Nepsis, this helpful practice, resonates with us yet again.

There is no one-solution-fits-all formula that we can use in terms of the amount of food per day one should consume. For example, there is no way I need to be eating as much as an Olympic athlete. We all come in different shapes, sizes, colors, sexes, ethnicities, ages, etc., and we all need to find the amount of food our body needs to be in balance, to manage weight, and to prevent chronic diseases.

Eating healthfully and mindfully involves much more than calories in versus calories out. A great deal of research indicates that when a person eats more than his or her body needs, chronic inflammation can be created in the body that could potentially be the cause of many diseases such as diabetes, heart disease, and cancers.

> *You must teach yourself how to eat less, but with discernment, insofar as your work allows. The measure of temperance should be such that after lunch you want to pray.*
>
> —St. Silouan the Athonite

Many of the Holy Fathers also speak to this issue of overeating. They note that when we have too much food, it can weigh us down and make us tired, interfering with our spiritual work, acts of charity, and prayer.

Saint Gregory of Sinai (born in the 1260s) offers this insight on eating: "The way to eat that is free from sin and pleasing to God has three degrees: abstinence, adequacy, and satiety." He goes on to explain, "To abstain means to remain a little hungry after eating; to eat adequately means neither to feel hungry nor weighed down. But eating beyond satiety is the door to gluttony, through which lust comes in."

Training Tool

In the box below, define the state in which you usually leave the meal table after you finish eating. What do you think is influencing it? In your assessment, consider the just-mentioned three degrees of eating of Saint Gregory:

» Abstinence
» Adequacy
» Satiety

SECTION 3

The 80/20 Rule

We need to become masters of leaving the table more often than not in the adequacy zone. But at the same time, we need to be able to accept and learn from our falls.

Saint John of the Ladder speaks to this: "Do not be surprised that you fall every day; do not give up, but stand your ground courageously. And assuredly, the angel who guards you will honor your patience."

Let's try looking at our approach to eating using the 80/20 rule. About 80 percent of the time, we're on track—eating real foods *and* controlling portions. Then 20 percent of the time, things get a little off track. We might have that extra bite of steak or chocolate cake that we know our body didn't need—the over-the-edge bite.

Another scenario could be that we're eating somewhere away from home and have no control over the food being served. The foods may not have been prepared with real ingredients. This will happen. And that's okay. It's one meal out of more than a thousand meals we partake of throughout the year.

Our goal is, as much as possible, to take control of eating in balance. The 80/20 rule is a good guide for this.

Pacing Ourselves Will Pare Down Our Portions

We have been given our senses to commune with the Divine. God in His wisdom created us to enjoy our food. Enjoying food creates an opportunity to be grateful.

Picture this scenario. You accidentally touch a hot plate. Within milliseconds your finger's nerve receptors trigger an automatic message to your brain, and you instantly pull your hand away.

Yet it takes at least fifteen to twenty minutes for your stomach to send a message up to your brain that you've had enough to eat. Maybe God's master plan was to create this time for respite in the day, leading us to sit and savor our time with Him.

It's as if this opportunity has been given to us, inviting us to partake in His marvelous creation through the act of savoring foods from His earth. It's time to "dine with the Divine."

> *One of the very nicest things about life is the way we must regularly stop whatever it is we are doing and devote our attention to eating.*
>
> —Luciano Pavarotti

And as we do, what a joy it would be if the words from the Akathist Hymn "Glory to God for All Things" would touch and soothe our thoughts and prayers: "Glory to Thee for each different taste of berry and fruit."

Training Tool

In the box below, indicate—using an average in minutes—the length of time you spend on every meal.

Breakfast: _______

Lunch: _______

Dinner: _______

SECTION 4

Savoring Our Food

Let's take a moment and picture ourselves dining with Christ Himself. What type of meal would we want to prepare for Him? What type of conversation would we want to have? How would we want to serve Him? Where would we want to partake of the meal? When we dine, we dine with Christ. Christ is in our midst; He is and ever shall be.

Research demonstrates over and over again, the faster we eat the more we eat. When we slow down our eating pace, we get to taste and savor our food. If we're looking at eating as a time to give thanks and partake in God's creation, we should not want to rush. We should set ourselves up to cherish the moment of mealtime.

When we eat at a fast pace, we do not taste our food. Taste buds are on the tongue, not in the stomach, so there is no rush for those bites to make it down there. We should take our time and allow the food to caress the taste buds that are screaming for interactions with food and drink.

Here's something we might be wise to try: Eat one meal blindfolded. Let's allow ourselves to pay attention to the taste, texture, and flavors of the food. Moreover, when we eat with a blindfold on, we will find it is a major challenge to eat fast. Hence it's a great exercise to aid us in slowing down our eating pace.

> *We load up on oat bran in the morning so we'll live forever. Then we spend the rest of the day living like there's no tomorrow.*
>
> —Lee Iacocca

If we're eating with Christ, would we want to rush through our meal in order to move on to the next task in our day? God is with us. He is there and everywhere. We just fail to acknowledge His omnipresence in our life. In fact, we hear of His ever-presence in our prayers:

> O Heavenly King, Comforter, the Spirit of Truth, who are everywhere present and fill all things; Treasury of Blessings, and Giver of Life—Come and dwell in us, and cleanse us from every impurity, and save our souls, O Good One.

Eating is a break in the day, a special time to commune with God. Now let's pause for a moment and think about eating by asking these two questions: Do you like food because you're fond of that uncomfortable feeling of being stuffed? Or do you like food because of the way it tastes?

If you answered "because of the way it tastes," then you should start getting in the habit of eating slowly—slowly enough so you can taste your food. I think if I did have Christ at my dinner table and we were sharing a meal, I could not thank Him enough for making eating enjoyable.

"Thank you, Lord," I'd say, "for giving us a sense of smell and taste buds that invigorate our enjoyment of food."

Enjoying a good meal and savoring every bite makes me think of this quote from the German theologian Meister Eckhart: "If the only prayer you said in your whole life was, 'thank you,' that would suffice."

I often feel humbled by the thought that not only do I have the ability to taste, but I also have the blessing of being able to choose what I am going to eat. We know this is not the case for all people throughout our world.

If we look at every meal as a gift, we can change our relationship with our food in such a way that eating becomes a grace-filled event.

Training Tool

In the box on the next page, indicate one of your favorite foods. Now think about the last time you enjoyed it.

» How did you feel about your level of gratitude toward that food?

» What can you do to bring a greater appreciation to meal time?

» When you enjoyed that food, did you take the over-the-edge bite? This is a helpful question in light of our recent discussion that we enjoy food because of the way it tastes—and not because we enjoy the uncomfortable feeling of being full. Reflecting on this may help us to be mindful the next time we enjoy one of our favorite foods.

SECTION 5

Controlling Portion Size

Now let's look at some strategies to assist us in controlling the portion size of meals and making mealtime a time to commune with God.

Whenever we sit down to eat, we must always remember: It's a time to eat—not a time to overeat. It's a time for us to clock out of the day, to let go of our long lists, and to focus on using our senses to commune with the Divine.

It is a time to give thanks!

Training Tool

Here are some strategies and suggestions to help us work toward slowing down our eating pace:

» Try to always be the last one finished at the table.

» Try eating a meal with your non-dominant hand.
» Try eating a variety of meals with chopsticks, especially if using them is not your forte.
» At dinner, set a timer to help you pace yourself. Set it for 15 minutes, and at 15 minutes, your goal should be to still have something on your plate.
» Remind yourself that you enjoy food because of the way it tastes, and when you slow down, you taste your food and that provides enjoyment of the meal.
» You do not enjoy that uncomfortable feeling of being too full, so your goal is never to take the over-the-edge bite.
» Put your eating utensil down every once in a while.
» If at meal time you notice that you took the first couple of bites really fast, create an eating break. Maybe remove your hands from the table for a bit and just take a moment to reset the eating-pace button.

In the box below, indicate when you feel it will be the biggest challenge to slow down the eating pace. What can you do to make it happen?

SECTION 6

Portioning Out Our Plates

We all know that dreaded over-the-edge bite. It's the bite that officially ruins the meal. We leave the table feeling uncomfortably stuffed, tired, and irritated with a bellyache.

Saint John Chrysostom, way back in the third century, advised us, "Eat just enough to alleviate your hunger."

In a recent study conducted at Cornell University, researchers demonstrated that adults eat an average of 92 percent of what they put on their plates. That means if we put more on our plates than our body needs, we're likely to eat it and take those few extra bites our body has no need for—just because the food is in front of us. Dr. Brian Wansink, author of *Mindless Eating: Why We Eat More Than We Think*, notes that this study is very helpful because "Just knowing that you're likely to consume almost all of what you serve yourself can help you be more mindful of appropriate portion size."[15]

A good exercise in self-control would be to put less food on our plate than we think we want. We can always go back for more if we really need it. The point to remember, though, is that if it is in front of us, we will probably eat it; so we need to practice discipline at meal time by serving ourselves a little less. We don't need to drastically cut our portions by serving ourselves half of what we usually eat. Just serve ourselves a tiny bit less.

Let's look at an example: If we usually eat 2 cups of food, we shouldn't go from 2 cups to 1 cup, but we should consider going from 2 cups to 1¾ cup. We should take just a tiny bit less than we usually serve ourselves or what we think we want. We can always go back for more, but the reality of it is that if it's in front of us, we'll eat it.

Dr. Wansink also demonstrates that when people serve themselves 20 percent less, they don't tend to notice the difference, but if they reduce portions by 30 percent or more, they realize it. A good way to portion out the plate is to serve ourselves 20 percent less in general, and go for more fruits and veggies and less pasta, rice (etc.), meats, and dairy. We should make the veggies the biggest portion of our plate. Remember, they are our building blocks. Allow them to be the foundation of the meal.

It's better to practice the step-down technique than to drastically slash portions. To illustrate, allow me to share a story taken from a splendid book titled *Greek Monastery Cookery*. The book reproduces a dialogue from the biography of Saint Dositheos, a novice monk. The dialogue is between the novice and his spiritual father, Abba Dorotheos, on the topic of disciplined eating.

When it was time for dining, he [Abba Dorotheos] said to him: "Eat and get full. Then just tell me how much you ate."

When he ate, he came up to him saying: "I ate one bread and a half."

The weight of one bread was four liters [*sic*]. Then he said to him, "Do you feel well, Dositheos?"

He answered: "Yes master, I feel well."

He asked him: "Maybe you feel hungry."

He answered: "No, master. I don't feel hungry."

Then he said to him: "Good. Then from now on, eat one bread and a quarter of the second bread. Break the other quarter into two, eat one piece, and leave the other."

He did as he was told. Then he asked him again: "Are you hungry, Dositheos?"

He answered: "Yes, master, I'm a bit hungry."

A few days later, he asked him: "How do you feel, Dositheos? Are you still hungry?"

He answered: "No, master. I feel very well, thanks to your prayers."

He said to him: "Then omit the first piece of the quarter, too."

He did again as he was told. Again, a few days later, he asked him: "How do you feel now? Are you hungry?"

He answered: "I feel well, master."

He said to him: "Break the other quarter of the bread into two. Eat one piece, and leave the other."

Again he did as he was told. So, with God's help, from six liters he gradually came down to eight ounces only.[16]

This story greatly exemplifies the step-down technique. When we cut our portions too drastically, we feel hungry; maintaining the calorie restriction will be difficult indeed. But when we approach calorie control through the step-down technique by serving ourselves a little less than we usually tend to eat and a little less than we think we want, we approach calorie reduction in a realistic way that can be maintained in the long term.

Training Tool

Regarding the step-down technique, it is a pleasure to quote my dear friend, noted author and founder of the company Mediterranean Wellness, Dr. Will Clower. He always tells people to serve yourself as if you are planning on seconds.

Next time you are serving yourself at a meal (and for future meals to come), put an amount of food on your plate that you'll look at and think: This will not quite be enough. Then take your time and enjoy that amount of food.

SECTION 7

Perception and Plating Your Food

I cannot resist sharing a story included in Dr. Brian Wansink's book *Mindless Eating.* (I chuckle every time I read the story.) An antiques dealer told him that when people who shop for antique plates find a pattern they like, they often take the dinner plate up to him and say, "I like these cute little salad plates. Do you have matching dinner plates?"[17]

It's funny because it's true. When dinner plates are smaller, it helps to control the amount of food we initially put in front of us. Back in the day, the plates, bowls, and cups were simply smaller. Now many of them are the size of a bathtub.

Take a look at the graphic below and answer the questions:

The Size-Contrast Illusion:

The Horizontal-Vertical Illusion:

Which dot is bigger?

Which line is longer?

Interestingly enough, the black dots are the same size and the lines are the same length. Yet this is a great example that illustrates our perception. When we place a sensible portion on a large plate, we look at that amount of food and think there is no way that is going to be enough, because the size of the plate makes the serving look small.

However, when we take that same amount of food and place it on a smaller plate, the plate-to-food ratio goes down, and it appears to be a substantial portion size.

Starting today, let's begin to use smaller plates, bowls, and cups. This is a good way to initially help us serve ourselves less.

Research demonstrates this over and over. In fact, Dr. Wansink conducted another study. Nutrition professors and doctoral students in nutrition were invited to what they thought was a celebration of a film project. But it was actually no celebration at all; it was an undercover, incognito experiment.

When the guests arrived, they were given either 17-ounce bowls or 34-ounce bowls. Then they were encouraged to take as much from four different types of ice cream as they wanted.

Those who were given the bigger bowls—and remember, these are people who work and study in the field of nutrition—dished out more ice cream: the equivalent of 31 percent more, which totaled 127 additional calories.[18]

To me, the lesson of this experiment is this: We need to stop before we start. To stop the temptation of over-serving ourselves, we need to start by using smaller plates, bowls, and cups.

Training Tool

What do you have to do in your home setting to make eating and drinking out of smaller plates, bowls, and cups happen?

This does not have to be an expensive endeavor; in fact some of my favorite pieces of functional art—my small plates—were finds at my local Goodwill store.

SECTION 8

Eat to the Point of Satisfaction

The early Church Fathers teach us that not eating past the point of satisfaction is where we need to be, as much as possible.

Saint John Cassian (fourth century) explains: "They [the Holy Fathers] have not given us only a single rule for fasting or a single standard and measure for eating, because not everyone has the same strength; age, illness, or delicacy of body create differences. But they have given us all a single goal: to avoid overeating and the filling of our bellies."

Today, let's start to implement this teaching before we even take the first bite. Let's become mindful of how we portion out our plates.

What do we do when there are a few bites left on our plates and we feel satisfied? You may say, "There are only a few bites left." We all know these bites. These are the bites we've heard about all our lives. I can still hear my mom telling me, "Rita, there are people starving all over the world! Please just finish everything on your plate."

> *If we eat those last few bites on our plate because we do not want to waste the food, we must still look at it as wasting the food.*
>
> *Eating more than our body needs is still a form of waste. Instead of actually tossing the food into the rubbish can, we become the rubbish can.*

As a young girl, I remember thinking, How are these last few bites going to help those people?

What we have to remember is that when we're satisfied, we're satisfied, and whether it's an extra bite or an extra three bites, it's still more than our body needs.

Instead of us throwing away those extra bites into the rubbish can, our bodies become the rubbish can. So really, in the end, we're still wasting the food—eating more than our body needs is still a form of waste.

The more we start by serving ourselves less, the less food

we will be wasting. We will cease to eat solely because the food is in front of us; neither will we have to throw out the extra food.

Focus on serving yourself a little less food than you think you want or than you usually serve yourself.

Training Tool

In the box below, describe what you will do to decrease food waste, whether it be in the form of throwing food away or of eating more than your body needs.

Here is a wonderful teaching by Bishop Platon of Kostroma, Russia. He provides us with a great exercise for mealtime: "At dinner," he writes in his *Rules of the Pious Life*, "picture to yourself the image of our Heavenly Father opening His hand in order to feed you; never omit your prayer before you eat, and leave some of your food for the poor."

Then he adds, "After dinner consider yourself one of the five thousand who were miraculously fed by Jesus Christ; thank Him from your heart and pray that He not leave you without heavenly food, His word and His most Precious Body and Blood."[19]

Bishop Platon's comments remind us of what we have explored so far regarding sacred eating, a pervasive theme in this little book. We've also looked at the importance of examining the components in the food we eat, emphasizing the need to eat food that will truly nourish us—and to be mindful of the portions we eat. Cutting down our portions does indeed contribute to healthy eating.

Now we move to the hidden blessings of fasting.

Michael, a participant in a "Food, Faith, and Fasting" workshop, shares: "I stopped consuming any food that had artificial ingredients, I ate slower, I consumed smaller portions, and I eliminated almost all sweets from my diet. As a result, I lost 20 pounds so that I'm close to my ideal weight, and I stopped having acid reflux problems that had plagued me for several years. Though I'm not perfectly disciplined with my diet, I believe I'm much closer toward "offering my body to Him as an instrument of righteousness" (Romans 6:13).

CHAPTER FOUR

The Blessing of Fasting

In this chapter, we will look at the different dimensions of fasting. An entire book could be written on the fasting tradition, but here we will briefly discuss the practice of fasting and its abundant rewards.

In the Sermon on the Mount, our Lord teaches us about prayer and fasting. Many of us recall the prayer aspect of that teaching, but we overlook the fasting. Yet there are blessings in fasting that we can experience if we fast for the right reasons and in the correct ways.

> *In the New Testament fasting is recommended as a means of preparing the mind and the heart for divine worship, for long prayer, for rising from the earthly, and for spiritualization.*
>
> —Saint Nectarios of Aegina

For those who are new to fasting, I hope this section will encourage you to incorporate this discipline into your spiritual practice. And for those who currently fast, I hope this section will aid you in enriching and deepening your practice of this age-old discipline.

SECTION 1

An Overview of Orthodox Fasting

Moses the lawgiver fasted; David the king fasted; Christ fasted; the apostles fasted; and we fast. Fasting is a timeless discipline.

The New Testament refers to attitudes and principles about fasting but does not detail specific days and foods. Fasting in the Orthodox Church, as we currently know and practice it, has been passed down through Holy Tradition. *Tradition* in the early Christian Church referred to a revelation that was made by God and was delivered to His faithful people through the mouths of His prophets and apostles.

It is a Jewish custom to fast as an act of devotion to God. The early Christians were Jews, and they were accustomed to fasting on Mondays and Thursdays. Then when they became Christians, they took this practice with them and changed it a bit to fit their new Christian context. They started fasting on Wednesdays and Fridays. Wednesday was in remembrance of the betrayal of our Lord, and Friday was in remembrance of His voluntary crucifixion. Still to this day, the Orthodox Church upholds this practice of weekly fasting.

From the beginning of Christianity, Sunday has always been the Lord's Day. It is commemorated as a day of celebration because this is the day of our Lord's Resurrection.

From ancient Christian times until now, fasting was not practiced in its fullness on Sundays. In fact, if the Church is in an extended fasting period (which we will discuss shortly), leniency on Sundays is always the guideline.

The Multifaceted Approach to Fasting

Fasting is much more than just abstaining from foods. When we refer to fasting in the Eastern Orthodox Tradition, we are referring to both the physical and the spiritual fast. In the words of Holy Hierarch Basil the Great (of the fourth century):

> There is both a physical and a spiritual fast. In the physical fast the body abstains from food and drink. In the spiritual fast, the faster abstains from evil intentions, words, and deeds. One who truly fasts abstains from anger, rage, malice, and vengeance. One who truly fasts abstains from idle and foul talk, empty rhetoric, slander, condemnation, flattery, lying, and all manner of spiteful talk. In a word, a real faster is one who withdraws from all evil.

While fasting, we use three aspects of our spiritual life to allow us to deepen our communion with God. These three are food, prayer, and almsgiving.

In food: We avoid the consumption of certain types of foods, and we decrease the amount of food consumed. In prayer: We commit to spending more time in prayer. In almsgiving: We spend more time helping those in need, giving from a willing spirit and a loving heart. (For the majority of this chapter we are going to discuss the food aspect of fasting; we'll explore prayer and almsgiving in a later chapter.)

The Purpose of Fasting

The tradition of the Eastern Orthodox Church has always seen fasting as a tool to combat the passions and to open the door to the renewal of the Holy Spirit. In this sense, the Church is viewed as a hospital for our souls. We heal the wounds of our souls with the many different "medicines" (disciplines) the Church offers, and fasting is one of those prescriptions.

> *Do you fast? Then feed the hungry, give drink to the thirsty, visit the sick, do not forget the imprisoned, have pity on the tortured, comfort those who grieve and who weep, be merciful, humble, kind, calm, patient, sympathetic, forgiving, reverent, truthful, and pious, so that God might accept your fasting and might plentifully grant you the fruits of repentance. Fasting of the body is food for the soul.*
> —St. John Chrysostom

St. Innocent of Alaska (1797–1879), in his work *Indication of the Way into the Heavenly Kingdom*, offers us this teaching about what fasting is and why it is necessary:

> Fasting is a voluntary self-restriction in food, drink, and pleasure. The purpose of fasting is to quiet or calm and lighten the body and to make it obedient to the soul. Overfilled flesh demands comfort and rest, disposing us to laziness, which hinders prayer and meditation. In the manner of an unbridled servant, the well-fed body rises up against its master, the soul, and wants to rule over it. While fasting, you should limit not only the type of food (dairy and meat products) but also its amount, restricting yourself to the minimal needs of the body. Then your fasting will become useful.

> *Man shall not live by bread alone, but by every word that proceeds from the mouth of God.*
> (MATTHEW 4:4)

Fasting has remained an act of dedication to the will of God. We choose to empty ourselves of things of this world to allow ourselves to be more open to God's will for us. That is why the Christian Church at the beginning of its era adopted the practice of fasting, establishing guidelines for the duration of the fasts and for specific types and quantities of food.

Fasting also serves the great role of making us conscious of our dependence on God. When we are feeling a real bodily hunger, an actual tiredness and exhaustion, these physical feelings can and should turn us inward, leading us to a sense of inward brokenness and contrition.

If we always take our fill of food and drink, we can easily

become over-confident in our own abilities, acquiring a false sense of self-sufficiency. Such is the function of physical hunger and tiredness. It works to make us "poor in spirit," aware of our helplessness and our dependence on God's assistance.

Fasting and Feasting

As we continue through this chapter, we will come to understand that it is important to fast so that we can properly feast.

In Eastern Orthodoxy, celebratory days known as feast days are sacred celebrations that commemorate the day of a saint, a holy event, or a holy object. Often we fast for an extended period of time in preparation for a major feast. In a way, the fasting properly sets us up to celebrate this joyous time. We see that there are times when the Church's prescription (guideline) is not to fast, as we are called to be in celebration mode—PARTY!

The Eastern Orthodox liturgical calendar is alive, and every year we have a rhythm set for us that outlines our periods of fasting and feasting. That is done to commemorate things that happened in the past and are still active in the Church today.

There are twelve major feast days in the liturgical calendar (please see Appendix III for a list of these feast days and the fasting and feasting periods that are set around them). Hence, we have a rhythm of eating and living established for us. The act of eating, and of not eating for that matter, connects us to something deeper. Remember, we're not just eating to feed the machine. Through eating, we have the special treasure of communing with the Divine.

As mentioned earlier, in the Eastern Orthodox Tradition, we are called to fast on a weekly basis. St. John Chrysostom explains to us that the purpose of this fasting is to prepare us for the partaking of the Holy Gifts. He explains:

> For the pious Christian, Holy Communion is the sacred privilege of being in communion with God Himself. It is a sacred union of his own being with that of his Creator and Redeemer. Thus the pious Christian tries to practice the commandments of God year round. His repentance, confession, prayers, fastings, and almsgiving especially before partaking of Holy Communion are spiritual acts which bring him nearer to God.

It's helpful to have a rhythm of eating worked out for us, especially living in this modern culture with so many foods, flavors, and choices available at our taste buds' tips. In fact, people are constantly seeking such a rhythm through all sorts of diet plans.

In my field of work, I get asked this all the time. People say to me: "Rita, I would like an outline of when, what, and how much I should be eating." Humans need rituals; they need a rhythm. We crave structure and direction. Much of what the diet-seekers intuitively feel they need is rooted in the past and outlined in the ancient Eastern Orthodox liturgical calendar.

How Fasting Focuses Us

St. John of Kronstadt, in his work *My Life in Christ,* notes:

> It is necessary for a Christian to fast, in order to clear his mind, to rouse and develop his feelings, and to stimulate his will to useful activity. These three human capabilities we darken and stifle above all by "surfeiting, and drunkenness, and cares of this life" (Lk. 21:34).

The rhythm of fasting and non-fasting days helps us to focus on why we are eating in a particular way on a certain day. For example, not long ago, I was talking with a spiritual father and friend named Paul; he comes from a British background.

He shared with me some of his food-centered cultural treats, one of which was putting milk in his coffee and tea. Yet when he wakes up on a Wednesday and wants to have some milk in his coffee, he instantly thinks, "Ah, it's Wednesday; I'm *not* having milk in my coffee today." He says that's an instant reminder to turn him toward prayer.

Because we eat every day and because eating is a basic necessity of life, the act of eating and drinking can be an immensely powerful reminder that will help us focus on God first.

For over two thousand years, the ancient church calendar has provided us with guidance when it comes to eating. Simply put, it is this: "God first, food second." We use this aspect of eating (or not eating) to deepen our union and our communication with God.

The Degrees of Fasting

There are various levels of fasting in the Orthodox Tradition, but it is extremely important to note that the Orthodox Church never reduces fasting to a legalistic practice. These are guidelines that have been set out for us.

We are all at different points in the food aspect of our fasting practice, but if this practice of refraining from certain foods and amounts of foods is not accompanied with prayer and almsgiving, then we are highly advised by many Church Fathers and saints to just eat whatever we want.

> *Sitting at meals, do not look and do not judge how much anyone eats, but be attentive to yourself, nourishing your soul with prayer.*
>
> —St. Seraphim of Sarov

Abba Hyperechius, one of the Desert Fathers, tells us, "It is better to eat meat and drink wine and not to eat the flesh of one's brethren through slander." And Saint John Chrysostom asks us, "for what good is it if we abstain from birds and fishes, but bite and devour our brothers and sisters?" Abba Isidore, a Desert Father, advises us, "If you fast regularly, do not be inflated with pride, but if you think highly of yourself because of it, then you had better eat meat. It is better for a man to eat meat than to be inflated with pride and glorify himself."

Let us remember all the aspects of fasting when we practice it. God does not need us to fast. In reality, God does not need us to do anything. We fast because we want to fast. We desire to put the tools of purification to work to bring us into closer union with Him.

You might be well-advised to work with your spiritual father to come up with a plan for your fasting practice. Those who have recently become Orthodox are often advised by their spiritual father not to keep the whole extensive fast but maybe start by simply removing meat from their diets on fasting days. (This alone is a big challenge for many, especially because our modern-day diet has become so meat-heavy.) Slowly, as new Orthodox Christians develop in the faith and disciplines, they can take their fasting practices to the next level.

Let's reflect on where we are right now with our fasting practices, and let's think of what we can do to make this practice a deeper discipline.

If fasting is a completely new practice for you, it would be helpful to read the plethora of valuable websites and books on the Eastern Orthodox practices of fasting. In addition, you may want to start by setting a realistic goal for your practice based on the suggestions throughout this chapter.

Orthodox Christian Fasting Guidelines

» Meat, dairy, and eggs would be the first major food groups to move away from.
» Fish with a backbone is the next food to move away from.
» Alcohol and oils would be the next foods to avoid.
» *Xerophagy* is a Greek word meaning "dry eating." This is attained when all of the foods mentioned above are excluded and when intake of foods usually consists of boiled vegetables, fruits, nuts, and bread.
» Strict fast is when no food or drink is consumed other than water, if needed.

Note: These are guidelines. The Eastern Orthodox Church has never reduced fasting to a legalistic scheme that requires following dietary rules. Throughout its history, the Church has always held that these practices are not for all. If, for example, someone is dealing with a specific health condition or if there are other legitimate reasons, special dispensations are granted to the believer.

Training Tool

Take a moment and reflect on why you currently fast. Think about what resonates in a positive way about the practice and what you currently struggle with.

SECTION 2

The Fast Diet

The FastDiet, also referred to as the "5:2 Diet" or "Intermittent Fasting," has been getting a great deal of scientific attention. Recently a book was published on this approach by Dr. Michael Mosley and Mimi Spencer, both from the United Kingdom. The diet's basic approach is this: On two non-consecutive days each week—for example, Wednesdays and Fridays—a woman is encouraged to eat no more than 500 calories, and a man no more than 600 calories. On the other days, each person is encouraged to eat a normal number of calories for his or her body's needs.

In the introduction to their book titled *The FastDiet: Lose Weight, Stay Healthy, and Live Longer with the Simple Secret of Intermittent Fasting,* the authors mention how Orthodox Christians have been fasting for centuries; and interestingly enough, the 5:2 fasting approach is quite similar to the way Orthodox Christians practice the act of fasting.

How Intermittent Fasting Works

Now let's look at a simplified explanation of how the biochemical aspect of fasting works. To start this discussion, we must understand one fundamental concept about our bodies: Glucose is the gasoline that keeps us going; it is the main source of energy for the brain.

> *Fasting consists not just of eating rarely, but also of eating little. And not just in eating only one meal, but in not eating much. Foolish is the faster, who waits for a specific time [to eat a meal], but then at the time of the meal is completely consumed, body and mind, with insatiable eating.*
>
> —St. Seraphim of Sarov

Glucose is derived from the foods we eat. The body breaks down the food, and from that breakdown, glucose is made accessible to the cells. To put it another way: Our bodies need glucose to survive.

When the body goes for an extended period of time without regular food intake, the body must look to its stored sources to continue to provide the brain and body with glucose. Our bodies have three main storage areas:

1. Glycogen: Stored carbohydrates that are found in our liver and some muscles.
2. Adipose tissue: Stored body fat.
3. Amino acids: The building blocks of muscle tissue.

Our bodies will first use our stored glucose. When that is used up, our bodies tap into our fat stores (adipose tissue) and convert this stored fat into glucose for energy. When we follow the intermittent fasting approach, we fast just enough to get our bodies into their fat-burning zone without causing our muscle tissue to become compromised.

This 5:2 approach to eating is so effective that it has been shown to help with various areas of health, such as weight loss and reducing body fat levels; improving blood sugar and cholesterol levels; reducing blood pressure; increasing longevity; and reducing the risk of stroke, heart disease, and cancer.

In fact, Dr. Michael Mosley practiced the intermittent fasting approach for five and a half weeks. Before he started the trial, he had his blood sugar, cholesterol, and the hormone IGF-1 tested (IGF-1 is a marker for various types of cancer). His labs at the beginning of the trial indicated that his body fat was 27 percent. After the five and a half weeks of intermittent fasting, it had gone down to 19.4 percent, he had to tighten his belt two notches, and he had lost 14 pounds. In addition, his IGF-1 markers decreased by 50 percent. His blood sugar normalized, his bad cholesterol (LDL) went down, and his good cholesterol (HDL) went up. (This data is from the *Eat, Fast, and Live Longer* documentary.)

I trust we will all agree these are pretty astounding results. For five and a half weeks, Dr. Mosley was simply eating in the manner the Orthodox Tradition has outlined for us to eat. What we are seeing here is simply this: The reduction in the amount of food we eat on two non-consecutive days a week (our Wednesdays and Fridays) can have great benefits for our health.

Research continually emphasizes that simple reduction of calorie intake for extended periods of time is beneficial for overall health. In fact, scientists from the University of Southern California demonstrated that fasting for as little as three days can cause a regeneration to the entire immune system. The scientists explain that a fasting approach like this could provide some promise for those with a damaged immune system, especially cancer patients on chemotherapy.

The researchers explain their findings in this manner: Extended fasting causes the body to use its stores of glucose and fat for energy. Also during the fasting process, a

> *Do you fast? Give me proof of it by your works. If you see a poor man, take pity on him. If you see a friend being honored, do not envy him. Do not let only your mouth fast, but also the eye, and the feet, and the hands and all the members of our bodies. Let the hands fast, by being free of avarice. Let the feet fast, by ceasing to run after sin. Let the eyes fast, by disciplining them not to glare at that which is sinful. Let the ears fast by not listening to evil talk and gossip. Let the mouth fast from foul words and unjust criticism. For what good is it if we abstain from birds and fishes, but bite and devour our brothers?*
>
> —St. John Chrysostom

significant number of white blood cells (immune cells) get broken down. This decrease in white blood cells during the fasting period causes the body to create new white blood cells, essentially causing regeneration to our immune system. An added bonus: The body appears to rid itself of the damaged or inefficient parts of the immune system during the fasting process.[20]

It may be to our benefit to consider doing a three-day (72-hour) fast, possibly once a year. For centuries, many have done a strict fast of mainly water during Holy Week, from after liturgy on Holy Thursday to after the Paschal (Easter) Divine Liturgy. This period may not be exactly 72 hours long, but even if it is 48-plus hours, it will still yield health benefits.

In keeping with what we discussed earlier, why we do what we do comes back to the spirit of it all. We fast—and maybe choose to practice this discipline a bit more intensely during Holy Week—in order to deepen our communion with Christ, and then our physical health ends up reaping some benefits as well.

Let's Challenge Ourselves

Now let's expand on this aspect of fasting as a way to deepen our communion with God. We do not wish to embark on fasting as a tool solely for weight loss or health. Instead, we want to fast as an act of devotion to God; fasting is one way to fulfill our desire to attain a deeper union with Him.

Fasting is a way to empty ourselves of the things of this world and to be open to being filled with Christ, our true soul food. When we fast, we end up caring for both body and soul.

Let's make an effort to focus on meager eating, as this is the guidance we are given for proper fasting through the Eastern Orthodox Tradition. Through this practice, let's take note of the benefits it can provide for us in terms of deepening

> *There can be no knowledge of the mysteries of God on a full stomach.*
>
> —Saint Isaac the Syrian

our relationship with Christ. Then as a side effect, we will become physically healthier beings.

Again, we are all at different levels in our fasting. Some of us may feel comfortable fasting all day with just one meal at sundown; others may feel the need to have smaller amounts of food at two or three meals per day. Whatever state we are in is fine. The main goal here is to implement the discipline of having less food.

"We get out of something what we put into it" is a cliché, but often truth lurks in a cliché, and there certainly is a truth here as we apply this cliché to fasting. So when fasting on Wednesdays and Fridays and at other times throughout the year, let's focus on choosing from the list of fasting foods outlined earlier and challenge ourselves with where we are in our practice.

If you have been simply steering clear of meat during the Holy Nativity fast, you may, as a new challenge for the year, try to stay away from dairy products as well.

If you typically stick to the prescribed fasting foods but are always leaving the table feeling overly stuffed, ask yourself, "Can I challenge myself by focusing on eating less?"

For those who are new to fasting, a major challenge in itself may be to remove meat from the diet on Wednesdays and Fridays. All of us are at different points in our fasting journeys, but we can always deepen our efforts.

Training Tool

Document one area in which you are willing to challenge yourself when it comes to your current fasting practices.

SECTION 3

How to Make Fasting Work

On fasting days, we need to remind ourselves to use the tools discussed in chapter three in regard to serving ourselves less and slowing down our eating pace.

When I'm paying attention to the meager-eating aspect of fasting and look at the amount of food I'm going to eat, I always tell myself, "Eat slowly and make it last, because that's all you're having, Rita." When my bites turn into "nano-nibbles" and I'm eating slowly, I appreciate the

> *Hunger is the best sauce in the world.*
> —Miguel de Cervantes

pineapple I am eating that much more.

No one ever said fasting is going to be easy. Most of us have a hard enough time turning down food when we are somewhat satisfied, but turning it down when we're hungry (so hungry that we could eat a hippo, as the expression goes) is really tough.

Again, let us remind ourselves that the physical feeling of hunger is necessary. We need to feel this physical feeling as a reminder to turn us to praying more. So, contrary to popular belief, it is a fine thing to feel hunger; indeed, food tastes so much better when we are hungry. Not only is fasting good for our body, but it can be very beneficial for our souls—provided it leads us to prayer.

Prayer is one of the three necessary aspects of true fasting. On fasting days, we might do well to keep ourselves busy. It's hard to eat when we're doing other things. However, we can always pray when we're doing other things.

Some of us may want to make our Wednesdays and/or Fridays days in which we serve others. Wednesday could be the day we work as volunteers at the local nursing home or the women's shelter. And Friday could be the day when, as a family, we make cards for those who are sick. On both Wednesdays and Fridays, we could take our phones, go for walks, and call those who may need a little bit of support.

When we fast, we eat simply. This saves us time in the kitchen, allowing the extra time to be directed toward the areas of almsgiving and prayer. (Please refer to Appendix III for fasting meal suggestions.)

Properly Fasting to Properly Feast

As stated earlier, there are times during the Eastern Orthodox liturgical calendar that are set as fasting periods, and these periods occur prior to a specific feast day. An example of this would be the Nativity of Our Lord (Christmas).

Prior to the actual day of our Lord's Birth, we fast in order to bring ourselves into the right frame of mind to celebrate such a joyous event. It is a way for us to empty ourselves of the busyness of our daily lives and allow ourselves to reflect upon the coming event.

From the Nativity of Christ to the day before the Feast of Theophany (Epiphany)—the twelve days of Christmas—no fasting is allowed. When the Church suggests an absence of fasting, it does so because we are called to be in celebration mode. Hence, to properly celebrate, we must prepare through an extensive fast. (Please refer to Appendix III for specific fasting and feasting times in the Orthodox Tradition.)

When we fast for extended periods of time, we need to use the approaches mentioned earlier in terms of meager eating and specific food choices. And during an extensive fast, it is still beneficial for us to place a special emphasis on our traditional fast days of Wednesdays and Fridays by eating an even more meager amount of food on those two days.

In general, when in fasting periods, we should consider eating less than we tend to eat normally, and we need to limit our between-meal snacking as much as possible.

Training Tool

In the box on the next page, write down something you would like to change when it comes to your fasting practice. Write down what you expect to be barriers to your change and how you plan to overcome them.

Here are two examples:

I would like to start fasting from meat, dairy, and fish on the fasting days of Wednesday and Friday.

Barrier:

I would need to come up with alternative foods and recipes to replace meat, dairy, and fish.

Solution:

See Appendices II and III for fasting recipes and tips.

Seek out vegan meal ideas and recipes.

I would like to focus on eating less on days when I am fasting.

Barrier:

I can tell I'm going to feel hungry, and I don't like that feeling.

Solution:

Focus on taking your time and eating slowly during meal time.

Create some peace around feeling hungry, and have a prayer to turn to when you are starting to feel the hunger pains.

SECTION 4

Proper Feasting

As we have briefly discussed, proper fasting leads to proper feasting. We celebrate feast days throughout the year, and we should make this time a special time.

Just as the Church has passed down to us certain traditions, we also need to establish and cultivate our own practices that can become our family traditions. Making certain recipes and doing celebratory activities related to feast days is a wonderful thing to tie the act of eating and feasting into the sacred moment being commemorated.

I can remember my mom making special doughnuts that we would dunk in sugar syrup on the feast day of Epiphany. She explained to us that the dunking of the doughnuts was a reminder of Christ's Baptism in the River Jordan. Each year we looked forward to these doughnuts, but they were more than just doughnuts: the dunking would aid in commemorating the feast-day celebration as we chanted the appropriate *troparion* (a short sacred hymn).

Another tradition in my family is that on Holy Friday in the afternoon, prior to Christ's body being taken down from the tree, we take a tablespoon of vinegar. Yuck! I'd have to agree. But again, my mother told me that when she was young, my grandma would line up her nine children and give them each a tablespoon of vinegar before they headed to the Holy Friday afternoon service. My grandma used this tradition to teach her children about our Lord's voluntary suffering, remembering the vinegar He was given to drink as He hung on the Cross. I am thankful my mom continued to practice this tradition and also passed it along.

Another tradition commemorates the day associated with the Beheading of St. John the Baptist. His head was requested to be presented on a platter. So each year on this fast day, Orthodox traditionally eat only out of bowls.

Let's cultivate traditions in our home that will aid us in

connecting to the feast days and fast days we're celebrating. Here are some suggestions:

» On feast days before saying the dinner prayer, chant the troparion for the feast.

» Invite people over and make it a special party. Another form of almsgiving is to invite those who have nowhere to go. Decorate the dinner table in a special way.

» Get the kids involved and have them color specific icon pictures related to the feast or draw something about the celebration.

» Save a special bottle of wine to be uncorked on the feast day.

» Even if a special feast falls during a fasting period, we need to celebrate. One example would be Palm Sunday, which falls during the Great Lent fast; another example would be St. Nicholas Day, which falls during the Nativity fast. On Palm Sunday fish is allowed (and welcomed, I might add). Plan a special fish dish and follow it up with a special fasting dessert. Serve the special-treat dishes only on fasting-feast days. We appreciate a dessert or other special dish more when it is not always available.

Training Tool

In the box on the next page, document one thing you will do for the next feast day. What is this feast day going to be, and what is something special you plan to do?

SECTION 5

Be On Guard

Let's return to the tool of nepsis, for it can help us once again as we work toward a healthy lifestyle.

During fasting times, it is easy to get sucked into the many convenient and prepackaged fasting foods out there. Many of them are just processed balls of sugar and unhealthy fats.

Many vegans are quick to let you know that Oreo cookies are a vegan (fasting-friendly) dessert, and French fries are a vegan food too. When many people fast, they unfortunately turn to foods that are harmful to health. An example of this would be margarine. We are called to withdraw from the use of butter and dairy in general, and we often use margarine in its place.

We need to be on guard about this. Why? Because

remember, we don't want to lose the spirit of the fast. One of our goals when fasting is to feel hungry. We want to feel something different from what we are used to feeling when it comes to our daily eating habits. Butter is a form of fat, and it satisfies. If we replace it with something else that has the same effect, we may never feel hunger.

We also don't want to start giving our bodies foods that don't fortify them, foods that only set us up for more food cravings. Just as we discussed in chapter two, we want to stick to foods found in creation. This alone is the guide we should use when choosing fasting foods as well. The appendices include some recipes and tips for fasting days.

Remember that during the fast, it is beneficial for us to miss the enjoyment of certain foods. We gain when we lose—to echo the words of our Lord. And when the moment comes when we are able to partake again, we appreciate the festal foods more. The taste, the flavor, and the gratitude we will experience will not be the same if we're playing the substitute game (e.g., margarine for butter).

Training Tools

Think about current food substitutes you use when it comes to fasting. What can you do to remove the replacement food from the diet?

Examples:

» You stop using milk in your coffee and start adding a non-dairy, additive-laden coffee creamer.

Focus on enjoying black coffee for the duration of the fast.

- You are always seeking out vegan recipes and prepackaged items for vegan (fasting) desserts (examples, cookies, cakes, etc.).
  Limit consumption of prepackaged foods and sweet treats, and reserve them for special occasions. For example, if someone's birthday falls during the fast, commemorate it by enjoying a sweet treat to end a given meal, as opposed to having sweet treats handy and accessible all the time. Enjoy a small square of dark chocolate after meals. (When chocolate is 70% or higher in cocoa, it is considered a health food. The higher the cocoa, the lower the sugar.)
- You stop using butter and switch to a margarine spread.
  Try going without a spread altogether.
- You tend to consume low-nutrient-dense foods during the fast.
  What are some strategies you can use to limit this?
- You always have a bag of chips in the home.
  Instead of bringing chips into the home, have them occasionally when out.

In the box below, and in keeping with the examples cited above, list some food substitutes you use when it comes to fasting, and indicate what you plan to do to remove the replacement food from your diet.

SECTION 6

Breaking the Fast

As long as a fast may seem, the time always comes to break the fast. Shopping for foods to break a long fast should be a fun occasion for us. For me, bacon, cheese, beer, and a croissant (this list could go on and on) are treats I look forward to enjoying once again.

As you can imagine, when we break a fast, it's important to be on guard. This may be the reason there is much wisdom in the tradition that designates a fast-free week following a major feast day.

For example, the week following Pascha (Easter) in church tradition has always been a fast-free week. (There are others, and they are listed in Appendix III.) No fasting for the entire week; we are called to be

> *Conquer temptations by patience and prayer. If you oppose them without these, you will fall all the more severely.*
> —Saint Mark the Ascetic

in celebration mode. That's right, let the celebration begin!

Just this fact alone, of having a whole week to celebrate instead of just one day, I think, seems to help us avoid over-indulging or eating way too much. Nonetheless, the temptation is there.

Here are some strategies to help us be on guard and practice nepsis when breaking an extended fast. We need to fast properly—and to feast properly. We need to feast properly—and to celebrate properly. We need to celebrate properly—and to be in the proper spirit.

Feasting Properly: Some Helpful Strategies

» We should eat and break the fast with others as much as possible, as this helps to prevent secret eating.

» In addition, talking with others while eating is a way to slow down the eating pace. We should remember what our moms used to say: "Don't talk with your mouth full." We need to cultivate the art of conversation in order to slow down our eating pace at mealtime.

» We must not bring tempting foods in large amounts into the house. Yes, it's true: these foods do really develop voices. "Out of sight, out of mind" is always the best practice for this. We should not fill up candy bowls as that creates another opportunity to pick mindlessly.

» When eating at buffet-style parties, we should scope out the food options and decide to choose only the items we believe are made with real ingredients. It might be better to take small amounts of a variety of things, sample what we like, and decide what we would like for a second helping.

> *Without temptations, it is not possible to learn the wisdom of the Spirit. It is not possible that Divine love be strengthened in your soul. Before temptations, a man prays to God as a stranger. When temptations are allowed to come by the love of God, and he does not give in to them, then he stands before God as a sincere friend. For in fulfilling the will of God, he has made war on the enemy of God and conquered him.*
>
> —Saint Isaac the Syrian

» We should always start with less than we think we want. We can always go back for more, or even have the leftovers for our lunch tomorrow. Again, we must remember what we discussed in chapter three: If we put the food in front of us, we are likely to eat it. So we must plan our plates accordingly.

» We need to remind ourselves to practice mindful eating, and as much as possible to sit down when enjoying our food.

» If consuming alcohol, we must be aware that it may be a trigger for us to want to eat more. It might be better to pass up the pre-meal cocktail and have our drink with dinner. Consider having a glass of water between alcoholic drinks.

» We should seek out the smaller plates, bowls, and cups to use at parties.
» We might do well to pack our lunch for the next day with foods that were served at the party, so we'll know we're going to enjoy the foods again tomorrow. Just knowing this helps us not overeat at that actual meal.
» Cooking is a form of love! Many times when people cook a special dish, they want us to enjoy it so much that they end up trying to overfeed us. Believe me, I have many wonderful aunties in my life who should be on the TV Food Network! They never feel they can give me enough food. Something simple to say is, "Thank you, Aunty Maggie, I enjoyed the meal so much, do you mind if I pack some up to take with me to enjoy for my lunch tomorrow? I feel if I have one more bite right now I'm going to ruin the enjoyment of the meal I just experienced. I'll end up feeling uncomfortably stuffed." Sometimes it is enough for the person who prepared the food to know that you really did enjoy it. It's a form of love to show our gratitude for the meal they prepared just as much as it was a form of love for them to prepare it.

Training Tool

Do you feel you currently struggle with breaking fasts in an unhealthy manner? If you are currently not observing the fasts, do you feel at feast-day meals (holiday meals) you tend to overdo it? If so, what is something you think is a cause of this?

In the box below, list two things you can do to enjoy feast day meals in a proper context.

Having looked at fasting from several dimensions, and particularly as a way to aid us in improving our health in both the physical and spiritual domains, we now move to another phase of our journey. This phase is exercise and the joys and rewards embedded in it.

CHAPTER FIVE

The Joy of Exercising

Let's now leave the food discussion for a bit and focus on another area of life that has a tremendous influence on our health—exercise.

And on this topic, let's turn to wisdom from one of the Desert Fathers:

> Someone asked Abba Agathon, "Which is better, bodily asceticism or interior vigilance?" The old man replied, "Man is like a tree—bodily asceticism is the foliage, interior vigilance the fruit. According to that which is written, 'Every tree that bringeth not forth good fruit shall be cut down and cast into the fire' (Matt. 3.10), it is clear that all our care should be directed towards the fruit, that is to say, guard of the spirit; but it needs the protection and the embellishment of the foliage, which is bodily asceticism.'"

This is the wisdom of a fourth-century father. In twenty-first-century terms, this might translate into an admonition that exercise is good for your health.

We know that exercise supports us in areas such as:

» Weight management
» Preventing and controlling conditions such as diabetes, osteoporosis, and heart disease
» Blood-pressure control
» Management of depression and anxiety
» Boosting energy levels
» Aiding in restful sleep

Health is a multifaceted puzzle in which all the pieces are necessary and fit together—much as the body has many parts and all work together, playing different roles.

In short, exercise is not the answer to everything, but it is a vital piece in the puzzle of a person's health. Just as there is no magic food or diet pill, the same holds true for exercise.

There are twenty-four hours in a day, and even if we exercise one entire hour, twenty-three hours remain. The question now is, what are we doing in those other twenty-three hours of the day with the other pieces of the puzzle: sacred eating, food choices, portion control, fasting, and stress management (the topic of the next chapter).

Let's take a look at how this piece—exercise—fits with the rest of the puzzle picture of caring for both body and soul.

Mindful Exercise

Many of us expect exercise alone to be a remedy for overconsumption of food and drink. This thought process could lead to exercise becoming an unpleasant experience, especially if we fail to see the results we were expecting.

When we look at exercise in this way, we may end up feeling discouraged. But exercise is only one aspect of a healthy lifestyle. We must recognize that exercise alone is not going to solve the issue of an unhealthy relationship with food. Instead, it should be another tool we add to our "health toolbox."

As we have discussed throughout the book, nepsis is a tool to aid us in mindfulness. Nepsis, watchfulness, can help us practice mindfulness when it comes to exercise. It is a tool to aid us in nourishing our bodies and souls. In the twenty-four hours that make up our day, it's important to have a mindful relationship with food *and* exercise.

In a given day, various thoughts come to us that relate to food or exercise. For example, we may ask, "Is that over-the-edge bite worth eating?" Or, "Should I drive or walk to the bank that is certainly within walking distance?" We need to remember that analyzing—and responding—to our thoughts and actions in a wise and mindful manner is a way for us to care for our body and soul.

Being watchful over our thoughts in regard to overeating, laziness, conversations, or a host of other actions is a way to practice nepsis. The evil one at times will tempt us to eat too much and become lazy with lack of physical movement. He knows that when we feel weighed down from eating too much or sluggish from lack of physical activity, we will find it difficult to pray.

Unnecessary snacking or taking an extra helping at dinner even though we've reached the point of satisfaction might appear tempting. Watching television after dinner might tempt us to cancel a planned walk around the neighborhood. It is so easy to fall into those temptations and not be mindful of overeating and resisting the need to exercise.

Much as we did with eating, we need to look at embracing exercise in a different light. Exercise is a process, and it's a tool for us to use in caring for body and soul. It is not a tool to counteract overindulgence, but it is a practice that, believe it or not, can make overindulgence happen less and less often. (We'll review shortly a study that helps to illustrate that.)

We don't want to exercise simply to attain a desired look or to make us feel that gorging ourselves on food and beverage is acceptable. Instead, we want to look at exercise as another opportunity to foster our connection with the Divine. That is our first intention, and then, by the way, we may just lose those ten pounds we've been striving to lose, or we may get our blood sugar in better control.

Let's start by developing a healthy relationship with exercise. This teaching from Clement of Alexandria begins to illustrate this path for us:

> Physical exercise is good for the health. But not only that: while it stimulates the desire to care for bodily vigor, it stimulates the same desire for vigor of soul. Exercise is extremely useful therefore, assuming it does not distract us from more important activities.
>
> Some enjoy wrestling, others like to play ball in the sunshine. For some it is enough to go for a walk in the countryside or the city. If they were to wield a spade, however, they would be doing an exercise that is useful even from an economic point of view.
>
> The King of Mitylene would grind grain; it was one way, a tiring one, of practicing gymnastics. Other ways would be to draw water or chop wood.
>
> Wrestling, it goes without saying, should not simply be a matter of competition, but a way to make you work up a sweat.
>
> In any case, we must always keep a balance: neither doing nothing nor killing ourselves with exhaustion.[21]

Clement of Alexandria lived from AD 150 to 215. Amazing how relevant his teachings are for us in this modern-day age of twenty-four-hour fitness centers, treadmills, and stair-steppers. This teaching is relevant because we are all at different points with our commitments to exercise, but we all need to commit.

I have fond memories of the days I would visit a monastery and would have a special time talking with one of the nuns who did a lot of gardening. She would always emphasize how important it is for us to work with our hands. Be it gardening, carving, painting, sowing, or kneading dough, she would tell me that the Holy Fathers stressed the importance of the use of our hands.

Exercise is still a time for us to pray. It is also a way for us to take care of our health so that we can be ready and willing servants to our King. We hear this statement all the time: "To take care of others, we must first help ourselves." That statement reminds me of what the flight attendants say about the use of oxygen masks in an emergency: Adjust your own mask properly before helping anyone else.

Taking care of ourselves through exercise is a way for us to care for our health; and when we are healthy, we are in a much better position to help others.

When we look at exercise in a new light, when we look at it as a tool to aid us in caring for our body and soul and as a way for us to care for ourselves so that we can be there for others, we come to embrace the idea that exercise needs to be a part of our life. But we must approach it with the right spirit.

SECTION 1

Let's Make Movement Matter

In this day and age, we're sitting more and more and we're eating more and more. Back in the day, exercise was built into daily routines: gardening, churning butter, the two-mile walks to and from school. Now our days are spent sitting next to computers, televisions, and hand-held devices, and inside of cubicles and cars.

The good news about exercise is that it can and should take many different forms. This is great because it makes it more feasible to make exercise a part of everyday life. I'd be ecstatic if I could take long nature walks every single day, but that is not a reality for me. On days that it can happen, great! But on the days when that structured physical adventure can't happen (nor another physical activity I enjoy), then it's time to figure out other ways to sneak in the exercise. Now let's discuss how to do that.

Every Little Step Counts

Short bursts of exercise do really add up, and every bit of movement does count.

A former co-worker of mine who wanted to lose some weight would always stress herself out trying to make it to the gym after work. This went on for days, weeks, months, years.

I'd hear it over and over again: "I want to lose weight, I need to exercise more, I'm going to the gym after work," and nothing ever happened.

> *The devil quickly finds work for idle hands and an angel quickly finds work for diligent hands.*
>
> —St. Nikolai Velimirovich

We had many conversations about short bursts of exercise and how they do really add up. I suggested she take a walk on her lunch break and park farther away in the office parking lot, but she was not buying into that at all.

Then the day came. She decided to further her education, so she packed up her car and off to the Big Apple she went. The first thing she did when she moved to New York City was to sell her car.

In her new carless life, she had to walk to the bus stop, walk to work, walk to the grocery store, walk to meetings. Essentially, she started to create short bursts of exercise throughout her day. Within a month and a half, she was down ten pounds, without changing anything about her eating or adding any structured form of activity.

She was astounded at how walking—simply walking—more throughout her day helped her lose the weight she had been struggling with for such a long time. And yes, I have to admit: I bit my tongue and refused to recite that world-famous line—"I told you so!"

Another story that I think drives home the point (and one that I found quite humorous) concerns a foreign-exchange student from Russia. The student had the opportunity to study abroad and was living in an East Coast metropolitan area in the United States. She was getting ready to return home and was asked, "What is one thing you observed in your life in the United States that you feel is a bit bizarre?"

Her response: "I find it odd that people will drive to a given store that is a five-minute walk away, but then go to a gym and walk or run on a treadmill for an hour. Why don't they just walk more throughout their day?"

Something that was intuitive to her and part of her cultural upbringing seems so foreign to many of us. We don't consider it "exercising" if we live and work in a metropolitan area and walk to do our errands or to work.

We've been bombarded with many messages when it comes to exercise. It has been so promoted that some argue we need to do some kind of physical activity for one hour straight, and our heart has to reach x number of beats per minute for it to count.

All this has led many of us to surrender to that all-or-nothing mentality. "If I can't do something for an hour straight, I might as well not do anything at all." Yet this Russian girl knew that walking throughout the day is a form of exercise that does yield results.

People report this all the time. They will return to America from a visit to Italy or France and say, "Those people are eating such delicious foods, and they walk everywhere!" These cultures are always revered as models of health.

Yet for many of us living in the United States, walking so much seems like a foreign concept. We are living in this modern country that, it seems, was not designed to be walker-friendly. Even though this may be the case, we should still try to add some extra steps into our daily routines whenever we can.

Obesity expert Dr. James Levine from the Mayo Clinic explains that we should never sit for an hour straight, because when we do, our bodies idle, the gunk builds up, and the blood sugars and blood fats elevate. He explains that in order to keep the fuels moving through the system, we need to get moving every hour.[22]

Walking could be the simplest way to make this happen. Plain and simple: we need to walk and walk and walk throughout our days as much as we possibly can. As long as we humans have had legs, we've walked. Why stop now? We need to create ways to add as many extra steps into our day as possible.

> *Walking: the most ancient exercise and still the best modern exercise.*
>
> —Carrie Latet

Here are some suggestions to get us on the path to walking more and more:

» Our tendency is to look for the closest parking spot to the office or a store. Instead, park in the farthest possible spot. Make this your normal parking routine.

» Take the stairs as much as possible. If you need to go up fourteen flights, take the elevator for half the way up and walk the rest.

» Find a buddy with whom to take a fifteen-minute walk

during a break from work. Holding each other accountable will help you stick with it.

- When on the phone, if you can, march in place or walk around the room. Make cell phone calls while taking a walk.
- March or jog in place or hop on a stationary bike when a television commercial comes on during your favorite show.
- Set your work calendar to ding every hour; this will remind you to at least get up and stretch or walk in place.
- Wear a pedometer and set a goal to increase your steps from one day to the next. There are many smart-phone apps that work as pedometers.
- Plan with family or friends to check out good places to hike in the area where you live.
- Take the long way to meet the kids at the bus stop.

Training Tool

In the box below, indicate two ways you can add more steps to your day.

SECTION 2

No Time? No Worries!

As we have already seen, short bursts of walking really do add up. The research emphasizes this over and over again.

A study was conducted in Ontario, Canada, at McMaster University, an institution that is leading the way with research in high-intensity interval training. In this study, researchers recruited fourteen men and women who were living a sedentary lifestyle and were overweight—but were otherwise found to be healthy. These people were also chosen because they stated that lack of time was one of their main reasons for not exercising.

In the study, participants rode on stationary bicycles. Each session consisted of a two-minute warm-up of slow pedaling, followed by three intervals in which the participants had to pedal as fast as they possibly could for twenty seconds, then pedal slowly for two minutes. Then they would pick it up again for twenty seconds until three intervals were completed.

This was followed by a cool-down consisting of two minutes of slow pedaling. All that totaled ten minutes of exercise with one of those minutes (the three twenty-second intervals combined) being high-intensity exercise.

The participants repeated this session three times per

week, so at the end of one week, they had completed thirty minutes of total exercise. They carried out this regimen for a total of six weeks.

At the end of the six weeks, the results showed the group had increased their endurance capacity quite significantly—by an average of twelve percent, to be exact. They also had healthier blood pressure readings, and their effectiveness of burning fat increased. Better endurance and fitness were also noted. In addition, the males also showed improvements in blood-sugar control. Research continues to be conducted

Sandy approached me about losing some weight. She was eating well and knew lack of regular movement was her struggle. She said she would always bring her sneakers to work with the intention of going to the gym after work but would never go. She always came up with a good excuse for not going. We decided to have her put on those shoes for a 10-minute morning-break walk and a 20-minute lunch walk. She went from 0 minutes to 30 minutes of walking per day and noticed her clothes were starting to fit better. Within one month of walking more, she said jeans that never used to fit started to fit again. Doing these walks on a regular basis also helped her choose the stairs more often and park farther away. Essentially, she changed her thought-process when it came to exercise.

in regard to the health benefits of high-intensity, short-burst exercise.

Let's put the results of this study into practice in our everyday lives. On those days when we don't have much time, it's great to remember that a short burst of exercise—especially one incorporating some high-intensity movement—is beneficial to health.

If you know you're going to have a busy day, try taking just five to ten minutes (before you get into the shower) to do a burst of exercise that includes some high intensity. Examples: running in place as hard as you can; jumping up and down as fast as you can; or doing some squat jumps, mountain climbers, etc.

Indeed, this might be a great habit to create before every shower you take. Whether it be one minute or ten minutes of movement, try to make this your routine. This is a habit I have become accustomed to, and let me tell you that shower feels fifty times better after that small burst of movement.

Consider taking this practice with you wherever you go. You can do this if you're staying at a hotel, at a friend's house, or in your own home. Start today and make it your new pre-bathing (showering) routine.

Here are some suggestions for short-burst challenges:

» Fit in a 10-minute jog every other day and throw in one minute of sprinting (this can be in the form of sprinting for 20 seconds at a time).

- Get up early twice a week and do 5 to 10 minutes of strength training (weight-bearing). Research demonstrates when it comes to strength training, short bursts are little metabolism boosters. A little bit really does go a long way, and it all adds up. No need for fancy machines or barbells. Our own body weight is more than sufficient. Interestingly, Hershel Walker, a former NFL player, did a great deal of his workout without exercise machines. Sit-ups and push-ups incorporated throughout his day were among the ways he would physically train his body. Here are some examples of weight-bearing exercises:
    - Push-ups
    - Sit-ups
    - Calf-raises
    - Squats
- Take the stairs. (When we do that, we're lifting our body weight up one step and then another step.)
- Every time you take a shower, first do a set of push-ups and sit-ups.
- Do push-ups or squat jumps throughout the day. Four to six at a time, three times a day would be a good place to start, then build on this by throwing in another set or by adding a couple of extra repeats to each set.
- Take a 10-minute walk during your work day.
- Try this 7-minute workout, available on the web or as an app for smart phones: http://www.7-min.com/

Training Tool

In the box below, write down two ways you will add a short burst of exercise to your day. You can do different activities on the various days. For example, on Monday you will wake up earlier than usual and do some strength training exercises. On Tuesday you will walk or jog around the neighborhood. Just remember, any type of movement for any amount of time adds up!

Now let's look at some other ways to make exercise slip into our days. We should always remember: The more movement we make, the better—and it doesn't need to happen all at once.

SECTION 3

The Fruits of Our Labor

There are many ways we can make movement a daily part of our life. One simple way would be to use exercise as a way to attain the fruits of our spiritual labors, just as Clement of Alexandria illustrated for us in his teaching outlined earlier.

Here are some examples:

» Gardening (Nothing tastes as good as a homegrown tomato.)

» Shoveling snow (Yes, it's a chore, but whistle while you work, because it's exercise, too. You might keep going and shovel the neighbor's walk while you're at it.)

» Raking leaves (When was the last time you jumped in a pile of leaves? As you rake, remember to take in God's paintbrush; you might just find you don't want to stop.)

» Clean the house (Music is key for this! That broomstick can be a microphone too.)

» Coach a children's soccer team. (And don't just tell the kids to run around the field—get moving and run with them.)

» Walk to do your errands. (Even if you drive by the bank, choose not to stop; remind yourself this is a destination you only walk to. Also consider walking to the supermarket wearing a backpack. Fill the pack with your groceries and walk home. Thus the walk home will be a strength-training exercise, also.)

» Dance while the water for the dinner you're preparing is reaching a boil. (Trust me, it doesn't boil faster if you stand there and stare into the pot.)

» Volunteer for a humane society to walk the dogs. ("Woof

woof" is their way of communicating, "Thank you.")

- Take a meditative walk: clock out, relax, and rejuvenate.
- Do calf raises while you're pumping gas or in the grocery store line. (Yes, it's a conversation starter.)
- Do you have to go downstairs to get the laundry? Make it a habit to go up and down the stairs every time you have to visit the machines. (Stairs are one thing we should take as often as possible.)
- Do you take the bus to work? If so, get off the bus one stop early and make that your new bus stop. (Eventually this will become a habit, and you might even decide on a longer walk to take to arrive at your workstation.)
- Walk with a friend to release the stressors of the day. (Walking and talking—before you know it, you've walked five miles.)
- Encourage walking meetings. (Research indicates that ideas are stimulated, and it is a productive way to conduct meetings.)
- Teach someone a physical activity you enjoy, such as bodysurfing, golfing, cross-country skiing, swimming, dancing, etc. Share what is enjoyable to you and create health and happiness for another. Talk about a gift that keeps on giving!

Note: Just like with fasting, we all are at different levels with our exercise, and that is fine. If you have not participated in any movement for a long time, that is okay. The goal is to find what works with your current state and make something happen.

Some may have difficulty with the exercises mentioned above. These are general suggestions, but the take-home message should be that every type of movement does provide benefit. For those in injury recovery, consult your health-care professionals for exercises that are right for you. Some suggestions might be light weights and stretches from the sitting position.

Others may be dealing with chronic pain or disabilities, and stretches and water exercises might be the better option; here again, consult your health-care professional for suggestions. We are living in a time where the Internet can provide us with many helpful resources. You should be able to find some helpful exercises that may be appropriate for your needs and situation.

Still others may be experiencing the inevitable—age has settled in, and you cannot do what you once were able to do. That is okay! There is no one solution that fits all in the context of exercise. But we must always remember that some form of exercise is better than nothing!

Training Tool

In the box on the next page, indicate one thing you will do, whether from the list above or another idea of your own, to fit in exercise as a way to attain the fruits of your labor.

SECTION 4

D Is for Discipline

Remember, we're not trying to burn ourselves out here, but we are simply striving toward making regular exercise more of a discipline in our daily lives. As we have mentioned over and over, we are caring for body and soul, and physical exercise is a component that allows us to do just that.

> *Discipline is the bridge between goals and accomplishment.*
> —Jim Rohn

A word of caution: Do not set out to do too much, or the end result will be that nothing will happen. We see this all the time: The New Year rolls in, and people decide they will go to the gym every single day and then some. For the first two weeks, they are there every day after work; then all of a sudden, the reality that this is not a sustainable practice sets in. Nothing gets done, except the gym continues to make money off the no-shows.

> *Whoever prematurely begins a work that is above his strength receives nothing, but only brings harm upon himself.*
>
> —St. Isaac the Syrian

Let's discuss some feasible ways to make exercise happen.

Make Time to Move the Way You Like to Move

I am not a runner. In fact, the only way you'll catch me running is if someone is chasing me. As you can probably deduce, when I'm choosing regular exercise activities, running is not one that's high on my list.

Exercise can take many different forms, and what's enjoyable for one may not be for another. Let's explore the many different ways exercise can joyfully become part of our daily life.

Making an appointment with ourselves to do a physical activity we enjoy is a discipline and a challenge in and of itself. To say no to something else because we have this appointment with ourselves is not easy.

Let's look at our schedule for the week and see where we can pencil in a time—even if it's just 20 minutes—to do something we enjoy. Whether it's playing basketball, going for a bike ride, surfing, taking a hike, pushing the baby in the stroller, going for a run, or even dancing in our home—we need to make this appointment with ourselves.

Check out this bonus: A recent study conducted at Cornell University demonstrated that if we make exercise fun, we'll eat less after the workout. An experiment was done with 56 adults. They were led on a 1.4-mile walk. One group was told the purpose of the walk was for exercise, and the other group was told it was a scenic walk.

The participants all received lunch after the walk. Those who were told it was an exercise event ate 35 percent more chocolate pudding for dessert than those who were told it was simply a scenic walk.

The researchers followed this up with a similar experiment. Forty-six adults participated, and the ones who were told it was an exercise walk ate 124 percent more calories in the form of candy offered after the walk than those who were told they were on a scenic stroll.

Dr. Caroline Werle, the author of the study, stated, "Viewing their walk as exercise led them to be less happy and more fatigued." She also pointed out that the study suggests some people participating in exercise programs tend to gain weight because they reward themselves by overeating after a workout.[23]

What are we seeing here? Enjoyment of the movement we choose does count. If we don't like the stair stepper, then we shouldn't use it. We should make appointments to move and be active in a way that also brings us pleasure.

Training Tool

In the box below, enter an activity that you enjoy and note when you will make an appointment with yourself in the next week to make it happen. Write in the smallest amount of time you can commit to doing this and when the activity will take place. (Again, it does not have to be long. If 20 minutes is all you can do, 20 minutes is better than no minutes.)

If someone else asks you to do something, you simply need to look at your schedule and say, "Actually, I'm busy at that time; can we schedule it for another time?" We show up on time for appointments and meetings with other people all the time. Now we need to recognize that we need to make an appointment with ourselves to take care of our health.

SECTION 5

Try Something New

Another appointment we might consider making with ourselves is an appointment to try something new.

> *Every day I say to myself—*
> *Today I will begin.*
> —Saint Anthony the Great

We are caring for body and soul, so we can use this miracle of our bodies to do something that is not only good for our health, but also something we enjoy. If we never try anything new, we'll never give ourselves the opportunity to see if we would enjoy it.

Always wanted to try Pilates? If so, sign up for a class or check out a video online or from the library. If you don't like it, you don't ever have to do it again.

» Interested in learning some Irish jigs? Well then, get dancing! YouTube, your newfound personal trainer and dance instructor, is ever ready for you to search. It is a great resource for learning new dance steps. You might commit to a YouTube video a couple of times a week for an amount of time that you can make happen. Before you know it, you'll be throwing on some music and bouncing around the room with your new dance steps.

» If you never learned how to swim, it might be a splendid idea to sign up for a swimming class.

» There are many martial arts classes to consider trying. This may be an activity you do yourself or one for the entire family.

Whatever it is that's new to you in the context of exercise, make an appointment with yourself to make that activity happen.

Training Tool

In the box below, enter some new physical activity you are eager to try. Indicate when you will make this happen.

SECTION 6

Exercise Is a Time to Pray

Saint Basil the Great reminds us:

> Thus, in the midst of our work can we fulfill the duty of prayer, giving thanks to Him who has granted strength

> to our hands for performing our tasks and cleverness to our minds for acquiring knowledge, and for having provided the materials, for that which is in the instruments we use and that which forms the matters of the art in which we may be engaged, praying that the work of our hands may be directed toward its goal, the good pleasure of God.

Anytime is a time for prayer. St. Paul encourages us to pray at all times, "without ceasing."

A practice to develop in prayer is simply to ask God to bless any activity we are about to do. Whether we are putting on our running shoes or baseball gloves, if we simply make the sign of the cross over the object and say, "Bless, O Lord," we are practicing a form of prayer.

> *Make it your custom not to begin any work without prayer.*
>
> —SCHEMA ARCHIMANDRITE ZOSIMA

We should always try to make this a ritual in our life. Any activity, whether it is for work or leisure or a family activity, should commence with a simple prayer.

If we are involved in a physical activity that is quite repetitive and meditative, this is very conducive to prayer. A swim, nature hike, or bike ride is favorable for this. Yet prayer can be intertwined in our competitive sports too. Praying without ceasing means—praying without ceasing.

A fond memory of mine is watching the Pittsburgh Steelers

with my family. We enjoyed watching the player Troy Polamalu, who became Orthodox as an adult, do his job. He'd pop up from a tackle (that we were all glad to be far away from) and make the sign of the cross over himself. What a way to bring prayer into his work, which is also an intense physical activity.

Whenever we're involved in a physical activity of any sort, we should see how we can interweave prayer into the event. A simple prayer of gratitude after the experience is another way to make this happen.

Accountability Equals Action

On accountability and action, Saint Ignatius of Antioch says, "Train together, compete together, run together, suffer together, lie down together, rise up together as God's stewards, assistants, and servants." We don't have to embark on our health journey alone. Let's call on each other and support one another in the many ways we can.

The Buddy System

» In working out, try to find a buddy. A great idea is to get together with a friend and decide on what the workout goals are. Allocate points for meeting a workout task. These points can then be cashed in for prizes. Both people are doing this together, so you work together and encourage each other to attain the points. In so doing, you hold each other accountable, because if you don't have enough points, you can't cash in for the prize.

- Text back and forth with a friend throughout the day, encouraging each other in an exercise task we know might be possible for us to do. For example, we can do ten push-ups, take a five-minute walk, do ten squats, or move away from our desks and stretch. Simply exchanging texts (on what exercises to do) in the middle of the day or early evening may be that extra push that's needed to make it happen.
- Consider joining a group or club—a basketball league, a biking or paddling club, etc.
- Make an appointment with a friend or co-worker for certain days of the week to take a walk after work or on your lunch break. It is much easier to follow through if you're meeting up with someone else.
- Create goals. You might commit to walking a half-marathon or doing a 50-mile bike ride. Signing up to do this with someone else provides instant support, and when possible, you can train together.
- Many times people just need someone to organize an event. Take charge and encourage people at your workplace or church to participate in an upcoming 5K walk that might be a fundraiser for some worthy cause.

Training Tool

In the box below, write one thing you will do to attach some accountability to exercise.

Training Tool

We're humans, and humans like rewards.

List two things you will do this week in the area of physical activity, and if at the end of the week you have met your goal, reward yourself with something. It could be something you were already planning to buy for yourself (such as a magazine, a book, or tickets to a movie). But do not allow yourself to buy the reward until you have met your exercise goal.

Example: This week I will do a short burst of exercise before my shower for three days. If I meet this goal, I will reward myself with a ticket to the movies or a new kitchen apron.

We've now added exercise to our health toolbox. That box could easily be flipped over by stress. But there are ways—spiritual ways—to manage stress, and we'll look at them next.

We'll see what it feels like to stress and un-stress in the next chapter.

Anita, a participant in a "Food, Faith, and Fasting" workshop, shares: "While I know your class is not about being on a 'diet,' I must let you know that over the past year I have lost 20 lbs. I think one of the things that contributed to this was the incorporation of weight-bearing exercise. Also, in understanding my choices in light of my faith, I'm less apt to get too hard on myself for the failures, and I understand making these changes as a journey of my faith instead of in legalistic terms."

Lilo was granted the opportunity to study in Italy. After a year in his new culture, he was down 45 pounds. A large-framed 6'4" man went from 285 to 240 pounds simply by eating and living like an Italian. He said to me, "Yep, it's true: white pasta is what they eat, and living here my trusted automobile is my legs. We walk everywhere."

CHAPTER SIX

Buzz Like a Bee and—Be Stress-Free

We believe that we live in a stressful age. And in fact we do. In previous centuries, others also lived in stressful times. Stress is an ever-present and pervasive part of our lives.

Unmanaged, stress can have serious implications for our health and weight. Stress presents us with a good-news–bad-news scenario. The bad news: Unmanaged stress can have a negative influence on our well-being. The good news: Stress can be managed.

Through his extensive research, Dr. Hans Selye, also known as the father of stress research, proved that the relationship between mental stress and chronic disease does indeed exist. His research showed that harboring chronic stress is toxic to many of our bodily systems.

Studies demonstrate that stress plays a role in the causation of high blood pressure; in the development of infections such as colds and the flu; and in other chronic diseases, including heart disease, Alzheimer's, diabetes, and gastrointestinal disturbances. Poorly managed chronic stress may also cause unhealthy eating patterns, leading in some cases to overeating.

Stress may be considered as anything that is taxing to an individual. An event that asks a person to exceed what he or she is capable of offering or achieving is considered stressful. Stress is also anything that endangers our overall well-being or disrupts our normal routine, whether physical, mental, or emotional.

Now, this is not to say all stress is bad. Stress can have a positive effect in our lives. It can be a form of motivation—for example, a looming deadline. We can recall and visualize the deadline, and the deadline becomes a stressor. But it helps us to get the task done.

Stress becomes negative when it is extended over long periods of time and we're not putting forth the effort to manage it. When this happens, we become more susceptible to sickness, fatigue, chronic diseases, and food cravings.

We cannot eliminate stress, because the reality is that it exists in many facets of our lives. The aim then is to manage and improve our ability to handle the stressors that are a part of this earthly life.

SECTION 1

Understanding Stress

To better manage stress, it is helpful to understand some basic concepts about stress in relation to the body. To start, let's examine the two types of stressors that confront us: *acute* and *chronic*.

Acute: This type of stressor occurs when an immediate threat is imposed on the body. The body instantly responds. It is our body responding to an emergency situation. The body prepares itself for fight or flight (to defend or remove itself from the imposed threat).

Some examples of acute stressful situations are:

» **Mental:** Missing the bus; locking the keys in the car; having an intense work meeting

» **Physical:** Coming down with a cold; touching a hot plate; narrowly avoiding a major car accident

» **Emotional:** A visit from an unpleasant brother-in-law; having an argument with a co-worker; receiving the news of the loss of a loved one

Chronic: This type of stressor is prolonged. The stress response in the body runs constantly and may result in long-term effects on a person's health.

Some examples of long-term chronic stress are:

» **Mental:** An unpleasant co-worker one must deal with on a daily basis; poorly managed finances; overcommitting one's time; worrying about uncertainties

- **Physical:** A lingering physical condition such as an inflamed knee or uncontrolled allergies; chronic restless sleep; poorly managed conditions such as diabetes or elevated triglycerides
- **Emotional:** Poor home-life relationships; negative outlook on life; unhappiness with health; discrimination

Such varied types of stressors are part of all of our lives; they're not going away. It's how we choose to handle them that can make all the difference.

Training Tool

In the box below, indicate your two main current chronic stressors.

SECTION 2

The Stress Response and the Body

These gifts—our bodies—harbor the autonomic nervous system (ANS). The ANS controls functions such as blood pressure, digestion, metabolism, and heart and breathing rates.

The ANS consists of two divisions: the sympathetic and the parasympathetic nervous system.

» **The Sympathetic Nervous System (SNS)** is described as the "fight or flight" system: It is designed to help defend or remove us from danger. (It's our "stressed" system.)

» **The Parasympathetic Nervous System (PNS)** is described as the "rest and digest" system: This system maintains the stability of the body's internal environment. (It's our "relaxed" system.)

The ANS constantly receives information from the body or external environment, and these two subdivisions (the SNS and the PNS) work together to respond appropriately. When a chronic stress is imposed on the body, the SNS turns on and the PNS turns off.

Functions of the PNS include heart-rate regulation, blood-sugar control, and food digestion. The SNS elevates the heart rate and blood pressure. This happens because these bodily reactions cause blood to move away from digestion and aid in maintaining glucose in the bloodstream, which will then be used for immediate energy.

The SNS being turned on periodically in order to deal with an acute stressful situation is perfectly normal. In fact, this is how God fashioned our bodies, and we should give thanks for this. Take note, though: as previously discussed, when the SNS is on, blood pressure increases; and when the PNS is on, blood pressure decreases.

When the SNS is continuously on because we are not managing the daily stressors in our lives, it can lead to such physiological responses as increases in heart rate, increases in blood sugar, and a sluggish digestion.

To reiterate, it is normal for these SNS responses to occur every once in a while. But when the stress becomes chronic and improperly managed, forcing the body to continually have the SNS turned on, the body becomes taxed, and it may lead to health issues such as digestive difficulties, increases in blood sugar, and increases in blood pressure. When this is the case, we set ourselves up for many chronic diseases.

You may be asking the same question that intrigued me when I first learned about stress and the body: "Why does the body turn on the SNS for both acute and chronic stressors?"

This happens because the body is unable to distinguish one form of stress from another. The body simply knows we're stressed, and it reacts by turning on our stressed (SNS) system.

Nightmares illustrate this. When we have been awakened from a nightmare, our SNS is more than likely turned on. We may notice our heart beating faster, we feel very attentive, and our palms might be sweaty. Our body doesn't recognize that this is just a dream. Our body processes it as stressor, and as a result it turns on our SNS.

Our goal is to have the SNS turned on only periodically. When we're getting over a cold, we want the SNS on to help deal with this acute physical stressor. When we miss our bus and have to kick it into high gear and run, run, run, again we want our SNS on. When we're dealing with a crucial deadline, the SNS being on would be a good thing.

But when we fail to put forth the energy to manage chronic stressors such as work stressors, financial stressors, and home-life stressors, our SNS ends up being in response mode far more than we want it to be.

Soon we will discuss strategies that will help us have the SNS turned on only occasionally. I wish the stressors we all have to deal with would go far, far away—but as much as I have been wishing for that, it has not come true.

So I guess the grand plan, once again, is for us to work toward handling the stressors in our life in a spiritually minded manner.

Training Tool

In the box on the next page, refer to the two stressors you listed in the previous box, and consider answering this question: What do you think is in your control to start handling the two stressors a bit better? (Later in this chapter, we will discuss ways to improve our handling of stress.)

SECTION 3

Stress and Eating

Feeling hungry? If so, it could be because this chapter thus far is stressing you out! There is a strong correlation between unmanaged stress and an increase in appetite.

The woes of poorly managed stress:

- *Increase in appetite*
- *Decrease in digestion*
- *Metabolism does not function optimally*

We can start by remembering that our body cannot distinguish one stress from another. Let's say the SNS is activated. This is a typical pattern of what we can expect to occur:

Cortisol (the major stress hormone) and adrenaline (another hormone) are secreted. Then stored carbohydrates and fats are made available for energy. This release of carbohydrates and fats is a good thing because this makes energy available to make our body react in the way it needs to—for example, removing our hand from the hot oven rack we accidentally touched, or escaping the danger of a major car accident.

But when we allow the stress to remain unresolved (such as work-life or home-life stress), then adrenaline stays elevated and blood pressure remains high. Also, cortisol remains elevated and triggers the appetite to be stimulated.

To sum up: Chronically elevated cortisol levels stimulate the appetite. When cortisol levels are elevated every so often, this is fine; but constant elevation due to poorly managed stress not only causes the appetite to increase, but digestion and metabolism do not function optimally either. How's that for a triple-edged sword?

Still stressed? No worries: it's time we take control.

Taking Control

To a certain extent, we are in control. How we choose to react to a situation can determine how our bodies respond.

Something that is not in itself a stressor could become a stressor as a result of our reaction to it. For example, take traffic: Traffic doesn't make us stressed; it's how we respond to the traffic that makes us stressed.

If we're stuck in traffic and we choose to yell at the light (which, by the way, does not change faster if you scream at it), or if we decide to be frustrated with the person who keeps weaving in and out of our lane, then traffic becomes a stressor to us.

But if we're sitting in traffic and decide to turn it into the best possible situation it can be, then traffic is no longer a stressor to us.

We may instead choose to take this time to do what I like to call the "Smile" reflection list. Take a moment and give thanks for all the things up until this point in the day that have made you smile. It's such a good thing to relive those moments just through a simple thought.

My treasured friend Jacob is fantastic at encouraging this. He'll send me a random text that reads, "Rita, tell me one thing that has happened in your day thus far that made you smile." I welcome those texts, as they aid me in taking a moment to pause and simply give thanks. Gratitude is a form of prayer.

> *God gave you a gift of 86,400 seconds today. Have you used one to say "thank you"?*
>
> —William Arthur Ward

Robert Emmons, a psychologist at the University of California, Davis, and author of *Gratitude Works!* explains that many studies indicate gratitude can improve our well-being. It can help curb depression and anxiety, improve our cholesterol levels, and aid us in better sleep.

Yes, sitting in traffic could well be a stressor in our life. But it can also be a time to give thanks, a time to learn a new language, a time to sing our heart out, a time to safely chat on the phone with a friend, a time to have a story read to us via an audio book, a time to enjoy a beneficial podcast. (Comedic podcasts are perfect for a long ride home. A bonus here would be that laughter is a stress relief in itself.)

This discussion is a great segue into additional ways we can manage our stressors, so let's keep on de-stressing.

Training Tool

In the box below, if you spend time in traffic, indicate one thing you can do to make this a less-stressed experience.

If you don't have to spend time in traffic, take a moment to reflect upon one thing that occurs commonly in your daily life that you view as a stressor, and explain one thing you can do to handle it in a positive light. For example, you get frustrated with a task you have to do at your job. Can you play some music or think of your smile list while you do the task?

SECTION 4

Fatigue and Food Cravings

Professor Matthew Walker runs the Sleep and Neuroimaging Lab at the University of California-Berkeley. He and his team conducted the first study of brain activity in relation to food among sleep-deprived people.

During their research, the team observed that sleep deprivation led to more activity in the amygdale portion of the brain, which aids in governing the motivation to eat. The team also found that volunteers rated pictures of high-calorie foods as more desirable after no sleep than after a good rest.[24]

Numerous other studies back up this same notion of sleep deprivation and hunger. Such findings may lead us to evaluate our current sleep patterns.

If right now we feel we're restless sleepers who tend to snack a lot during the day, this helps to shed a bit of light on our situation. What do we see here? Food is not the problem; our failure to get proper sleep may be the problem.

Let's create some sleep rituals. Here are some suggestions:

» Keep the evening prayers by your bed (and say them).

» Hang an icon in your room. (Examples: your patron saint, Christ with the Holy Theotokos)

» Prior to falling asleep, bless yourself with holy oil.

» Don't count sheep; rather, count the things you were grateful for during the day and fall asleep reflecting on that list.

» Keep your bedroom free of electronics. Using a smartphone, tablet, or laptop at bedtime may be staving off sleep, according to scientists from the Harvard Medical School who have found specific wavelengths of light can suppress the slumber-inducing hormone melatonin in the brain.[25] Plus, checking work email before bed may get your brain in work mode when you want it to be in rest mode.

» If you do wake up, take this as an opportunity to pray.

» Keep a pen and paper by your bed. When a creative thought or a must-do task awakens you and you don't want to forget it, simply write a few key words that will help you remember the thought or the task the next day. Then back to dreamland you go.

» If you habitually snore or find yourself awakening with a sharp intake of breath, you may have sleep apnea, which can prevent you from achieving deep sleep (and in serious cases can even be life-threatening). Consider consulting your doctor to have a sleep test done.

Saint Gregory of Nyssa, who lived during the fourth century, helps us to see the importance of proper sleep even in these modern times:

The life of the body is one of flux and change. The human being cannot exist except in ceaseless motion like the flow of a river. To relax tension we have sleep. When we wake up, the motion starts up again. Neither of the two states lasts very long. But it is thanks to their alternation that we are refreshed. A constant tension would provoke a collapse: a continuing relaxation would result in the dissolution of the individual. The regular change at the right moment from the one state to the other is the secret of preserving human vitality.

So, if the body is tired, sleep takes over. Just as horses that have competed in the hippodrome are allowed to rest, so sleep is granted to us to restore us, relax us, and make us fresh for the new day.[26]

Training Tool

In the box below, indicate the sleep rituals you would like to try. What will you need to do to make these happen? Even if you sleep well, you may want to consider incorporating one of these suggestions into your bedtime rituals.

SECTION 5

Practice Positivity

Let's practice being positive by turning to, and learning from, the wisdom of the recently glorified Saint Paisios of Mount Athos. In a book published in 1998 by Holy Mountain, we read this story on the theme of positive thinking:

> I know from experience that in this life people are divided into two categories. A third category does not exist; people either belong to one or the other. The first one resembles the fly. The main characteristic of the fly is that it is attracted by dirt. For example, when a fly is found in a garden full of flowers with beautiful fragrances, it will ignore them and will go sit on top of some dirt found on the ground. It will start messing around with it and feel comfortable with the bad smell. If the fly could talk, and you asked it to show you a rose in the garden, it would answer: "I don't even know what a rose looks like. I only know where to find garbage, toilets, and dirt." There are some people who resemble the fly. People belonging to this category have learned to think negatively, and always look for the bad things in life, ignoring and refusing the presence of good.
>
> The other category is like the bee whose main characteristic is to always look for something sweet and nice to sit on. When a bee is found in a room full of dirt and there is a small piece of sweet in a corner,

> it will ignore the dirt and will go to sit on top of the sweet. Now, if we ask the bee to show us where the garbage is, it will answer: "I don't know. I can only tell you where to find flowers, sweets, honey and sugar"; it only knows the good things in life and is ignorant of all evil. This is the second category of people who have a positive way of thinking, and only see the good side of things. They always try to cover up the evil in order to protect their fellow men; on the contrary, people in the first category try to expose the evil and bring it to the surface.
>
> When someone comes to me and starts accusing other people, and puts me in a difficult situation, I tell him the above example. Then, I ask them to decide to which category he wishes to belong, so he may find people of the same kind to socialize with.[27]

To put it simply: Be the BEE! My husband uses this story as an analogy for his work team. As a group they are always reminding each other, "Be the bee!"

We should share this story (or a version of it) with those with whom we associate on a regular basis. As a group of people working together, we might do well to remember the wisdom of Saint Paisios and remind each other to always "Be the bee!"

Training Tool

> In the box on the next page, indicate one area of your life in which you feel you need to be more of a positive

thinker. What is one thought process you can change to support this effort?

Example: You get frustrated with a co-worker's negative attitude toward you. One time I was at a workshop, and the speaker began her presentation with this line: "Everyone has a story." Maybe you need to reflect on the fact that this person may have something going on in his or her home life that is causing pain, and that is why they act like this. It may make it easier for you to pray for them.

SECTION 6

All We Need Is Love

Christ called us to show love. In John 13:34, we are told by Jesus, "A new commandment I give to you, that you love one another; as I have loved you, that you also love one another."

If we feel there is no love around, we should simply share it, and then we will find love easily. The great thing about love is that it comes in many different forms. For instance, researchers have demonstrated many times that buying someone a gift can boost happiness in a way that spending on oneself does not.[28]

> *Kindness is the language which the deaf can hear and the blind can see.*
> —Mark Twain

Let's experience the joy in love and take care of our health at the same time.

Compliments Are Kind

Consider playing the compliment game. A small word of kindness (one of the many forms of love) can go a long way. When we give a compliment, it is like giving without expecting to receive.

We should create opportunities to compliment and, of course, we need to be genuine in what we are saying. Here are some ideas:

» Compliment a co-worker on her necklace or his shirt or on a job well done.

» Tell a stranger she has a pretty smile.

» Tell your spouse or roommate how much you enjoyed the dinner he or she prepared.

» Are you holding a grudge against another who thinks the issue has been resolved—or vice-versa? If so, find a genuine way to compliment the person and leave it at that. (The old expression might work here: "Kill them with kindness." Give that a try; you may be pleasantly surprised with the results.)

Attend to Almsgiving

St. Seraphim of Sarov put it this way: "Establish yourself in God and then you will be helpful to others."

Practice almsgiving. Almsgiving is a form of love, and remember, this is what we are called to do—and to do it even more frequently when we are in an extended fasting period. God truly knows what is best for us. When we willingly help others, it somehow benefits our health.

Throughout our lives, we will continually be dealing with strife and struggle. As we well know, this is a part of life that is never going away. But our approach to such issues can make all the difference.

> *Kind words can be short and easy to speak, but their echoes are truly endless.*
>
> —Mother Teresa

I once heard a story of a man who lived through Hurricane Katrina and lost everything. He was asked, "How are you dealing with the pain of losing everything?" He said whenever he started to get down about his situation, he would go and help another person, and it seemed to be a coping mechanism that worked for him.

An unfortunate yet helpful thing to recognize is that there is always someone worse off than we are. When our thoughts start to spin out into feelings of despair and hopelessness, it's important to turn to prayer and to lend a helping hand to one in need.

We can help someone by simply calling them and giving them a word of support; or by sharing lunch with a co-worker who has no one to eat with; or by giving money to someone who is struggling financially; or by volunteering to build houses for the needy. These are quick suggestions that come to mind. There are many other ways to share in almsgiving. Here are a few more ideas:

» Volunteer at a nursing home, hospital, women's shelter, soup kitchen, etc.
» Make extra food and share it with a shut-in or a friend who is dealing with a lot and lacks the time to cook.
» Babysit for a family to give the parents a night out.
» Invite someone who lives alone to dinner. There is much to be said for sharing a meal with others.
» Call a widow or widower and take him or her out to lunch or to some other activity. Many times these people are suffering. Life has changed; they used to eat and/or cook with another, and now they have meals by themselves. They used to run errands with another, and now they do them by themselves. Many widows and widowers have

a hard time reaching out, both because they are suffering emotionally and because they do not want to feel like they are being a bother. Take the initiative and extend an invitation. Or invite yourself over to their house with a home-cooked meal in hand. Chances are they will gladly welcome the company.

» Take charge of organizing some almsgiving activity that can take place on a regular basis through your church community. For example, take the lead on a semiannual food drive, or organize feeding the hungry on a weekly or monthly basis. Assess the needs in your community and perhaps lead a humanitarian committee in your parish. Others may want to serve but don't have the time to seek out options, so if we direct this endeavor, it could produce many fruits and an opportunity for others to serve.

Training Tool

In the box on the next page, indicate one short-term act of almsgiving that you plan to do this week, and then a long-term one that you may want to do on a more consistent basis.

Short-term examples: This week call a family member who needs some support. Or invite someone you know who is suffering from loneliness over for dinner.

Long-term examples: Volunteer at a soup kitchen once a month, or organize a humanitarian fund-raising event at your parish.

SECTION 7

Soul Food: The Purpose of Prayer

The purpose of prayer as understood in the Orthodox Tradition is to establish communion with God. We pray in order to know God and to be able to do His will. Saint Nectarios put it this way: "Prayer unites one with God, being a divine conversation and spiritual communion with the Being that is most beautiful and highest." Elsewhere he notes, "Prayer is forgetting earthly things, an ascent to heaven. Through prayer we flee to God."

> *Through prayer, man is cleansed, brightened, sanctified.*
> —Elder Amphilochios of Patmos

The Orthodox Church follows the Old Testament

practice of having formal or structured prayers throughout the day. Orthodox Christians are taught to pray regularly in the morning, at meal times, and in the evening. Brief prayers may also be repeated throughout the day under any circumstances.

Prayer has many different forms, and in prayer we see ourselves giving thanks and also asking. When we ask, we should always ask that God's will be done in our lives. Abba Nilus teaches us, "Do not be always wanting everything to turn out as you think it should, but rather as God pleases; then you will be undisturbed and thankful in your prayer."

Praying in this fashion allows us to surrender and trust in God. It aids in decreasing our worry as we submit ourselves to God's will. We humble ourselves and acknowledge that we do not know what is best for us; but what we do know is that we desire the will of God to be done. Praying in this proper fashion may also help to relieve stress. Much stress is caused when we try to control everything.

> *Try to make your intellect deaf and dumb during prayer; you will then be able to pray.*
>
> —Evagrios the Solitary

When we allow someone else to be in charge—that someone else being God—we take the day, month, year, or lifetime off from feeling like we need to play boss. When we pray in this proper fashion, we feel at peace with the end result, because we trust that it is God's will.

Another form of prayer we are called to practice is silence. We're always so busy telling God what we want; sometimes we need to silence ourselves so that we may hear the voice of God.

Prayer is not a one-way road. If we're traveling toward God, He, too, is coming right back toward us. Theosis is working with God. Through theosis God desires to share His energies with us. Silent prayer is just one of the many ways to experience this. Silence is a form of prayer.

Silent Prayer

Meditation in the Eastern Orthodox sense is viewed as a time for us to connect with the triune God. It is a time to silence ourselves and empty ourselves of the cares of this world so that we can become vessels ready and willing to be filled with God's love.

All forms of prayer are important and necessary; but silent prayer has a bonus that also benefits our health. To take this time to clock out of our day and just sit and be with God nourishes our body and soul.

> *Be still and know that I am God.*
> PSALM 46:10

Much as we discussed with the other health behaviors, practicing the action in the correct spirit is key. We're not practicing silence to benefit our health; yet it does just that. We silence ourselves with the intention of connecting with the Divine, and almost as a bonus, memory and other aspects of physical health improve. These aspects include cardiovascular health, specifically blood-pressure reduction. Silence also helps reduce symptoms of anxiety and depression along with relieving overall stress.[29]

Let's start today to cultivate the act of silent prayer. If you do not already have in your home a place where you can light a candle, reflect on an icon, and be with God, then you might wish to consider creating such a place. Make this place a place only for prayer. Don't write bills there; don't exercise there; don't eat there; don't even do homework there. This space is reserved only for prayer.

> *If you are silent, you will have peace wherever you live.*
>
> —Abba Poemen

Personally, when I've had a hard day of work and I meet up with my cherished spouse and he can tell I'm a bit frazzled, he encourages me to go to our prayer corner. I humbly go, although I admit it's hard to hear from someone else what I might need; yet in these cases, he's usually right.

I may sit there for five minutes or fifteen minutes, and that helps me to hit the reset button. Instead of taking my frustrations of the day out on my husband, I take time in silence just to be with God, and that helps me release the stressors of the day. It moves me into the evening hours with a more grateful and better outlook, allowing for a positive attitude that is conducive to love.

We need to create our own space. It's kind of like the adult "time-out" corner. Kids need discipline, and so do adults. When we commit to spending silent time in our prayer corner, we are disciplining ourselves, and this act allows us to say no to this and that—and yes to God. Our heavenly Father wants to commune with us if our hearts so desire. When we silence ourselves, we allow our Creator to do just that.

Now, of course, kids should be frequenting this prayer corner too. In fact, it's a good idea to have children contribute to the space. Maybe when we take a hike, the kids can pick some flowers to beautify the space. Or when the family comes together to pray, their job could be to light the incense or candle. This allows them to develop a sense of care and responsibility for this sacred space.

> *Prayer is the laying aside of thoughts.*
>
> —Evagrios Ponticus

The story is often told about a wise person who proclaimed, "Everyone should sit in silence for half an hour each day. But, of course, if one is very busy, he should sit in silence for one hour a day."

A dear spiritual father once talked to me about prayer. He explained, "If you have to fill up a basin with water, and you have two buckets to use, and one has no bottom and the other has a bottom with a few holes, which one would you choose?" Then he related this to our prayer life. He said, "It's better to pray with a few holes than not at all."

Maybe we can't sit for a half an hour in silence each day, but sitting silently for five minutes is better than nothing at all. Or, we may not be able to complete all the morning prayers, but it's better to do some of them than not to pray at all.

Our goal should be to create a prayer rule that we can stick to and manage. Yes, there will always be room for improvement, and the goal is always to pray more. As we hear over and over again, the more we pray, the more we want to pray—but we have to start somewhere to get to that point. We don't want to start by setting the goal too high, because that is a sure way to end up doing nothing.

What is our current reference point when it comes to practicing silence? If we are doing nothing, five minutes of silence two days a week may be a good place to start. If we currently practice silence inconsistently, we may want to implement five minutes of silence four days a week, and on certain days when we are able, expand it to ten minutes.

Training Tool

In the box on the next page, indicate one prayer rule of silence that you will try to implement for the week.

For example: I will practice silence for five minutes three times this week.

SECTION 8

The Rhythm of Life Through Sacred Reading

My creative friend Sheri puts her heart into teaching children about the faith. Every time I observe her teaching, I am impressed by her hands-on ways; she engages the children.

During one of her classes that I attended, she started the session with handing each child a present. The children were told that when she called them, they were to open their present and share with the class what was inside.

Each child eagerly and patiently awaited his or her turn. I sat there wondering what these presents were that were all uniform in size. Then the first one was opened, and the child pulled out a sheet of paper that contained a psalm. Each child opened a different psalm and read it to the class. Sheri then offered some questions to the children, and she discussed the psalm with them.

"Psalm 23," she explained, "is a psalm where we see love,

comfort, and nurture given to us by our Heavenly Father." (Psalm 23 is Psalm 22 in the Septuagint Psalter used in the Orthodox Church.)

Psalm 22(21) was read, and she asked the children, "Have you ever felt angry or in despair?" Then she added, "This is a psalm for seeking comfort and understanding when we are feeling like that."

Psalm 148, she explained, is a fine one to remember during those moments when we are so grateful to God and feel we can't give thanks enough.

Psalm 51(50) she explained as one that helps us deal with our feelings of remorse when we know we have done something wrong and we need to be cleansed and restored.

Psalm 46(45) helps us deal with our fears by knowing there is hope.

Other psalms were read. Sheri made the psalms so relevant to these children's lives (and the adults' lives). It was beautiful to see how engaged the children were when they were sharing their thanksgivings and fears with her and with the rest of the class.

> *Prayer is the fruit of joy and thankfulness.*
>
> —Evagrios the Solitary

The Psalms are therapeutic to read. They outline our daily struggles. In the Psalms we hear a rhythm of life: questioning God, crying out to God, and praising God. Our emotions are real. For the sake of our health, our emotions need to be processed, and the Psalms aid us in doing just that.

Sheri concluded the class by stating that the Psalms are gifts that have been given to us. (Hence the wrapping-paper touch.) We should cherish and use the Psalms to aid us through our days as we experience our various emotions and feelings.

Following the class, Sheri and I had a chance to converse. We discussed how the Psalms are gifts that have stood the test of time. People long ago were experiencing similar emotions and struggles to those we experience today.

In our current life, the Psalms benefit us through our struggles. The words are alive, and they provide us with hope and comfort. They are an outlet that allow us to communicate our feelings of anger and frustration to God.

These gifts, the Psalms, are sacred readings to incorporate into our prayer life. They are a healthy way for us to deal with emotions —struggling or rejoicing, questioning or consoling. Furthermore, they are written in such a way that the rhythm of the writings allows the words to vibrate in our hearts and throughout our being.

We should always try to read or chant the Psalms in our home on a regular basis; it is a good thing to do in our prayer corner. On certain days, we can incorporate a specific psalm into our prayer-corner time based on our feelings and emotions of the day.

Training Tool

In the box below, list a time during this week when you will chant or read at least one psalm in your prayer corner.

SECTION 9

Prayer for Self-Care

Unfortunately, at times, many of us find it difficult to pray. The demons know prayer is what is best for us, and so they work overtime to trip us and keep us from being steadfast and faithful in our prayer life.

A wonderful spiritual father with whom I had a lot of contact used to tell me, when you don't feel like praying, simply cross yourself, light a candle, and know that you are going to the best spa, because when you pray, you are communicating with God, and this is the best form of self-care.

Having specific prayers handy is a good thing to aid us as we commit to a prayer rule. We know what is best for us; now we have to create a plan to make it happen. As we have been discussing, things don't just happen. We have to work with God. We have to create some structure in our life around prayer, be it silence, structured prayer, or reading sacred writings such as the Psalms.

Just as we would have to make an appointment to attend the spa for that massage or facial, we need to make an appointment with ourselves to practice prayer. We need to make our appointment with God and book a time for prayer. Prayer is our free trip to the spiritual spa of true self-care.

Training Tool

In the box below, indicate one thing you can work toward this week to make structured prayer occur in your prayer corner.

If you do not have a prayer corner created in your home right now, indicate in the box what you can do to create one. Remember, it does not have to be elaborate, just a special spot to cultivate silence and structured prayer time. Here are some suggestions:

» Commit to doing your evening prayers right after dinner.
» Wake up 5 minutes early to have morning prayer time.
» When you come home from work, take just a few minutes to chant or read some psalms.

Celebrate the Services

Elder Joseph the Hesychast once wrote, "Man's chief aim should be to find God. In finding God, he finds true happiness."

We are hungry, although we are hungry for our real food. We need to seek out God's love through faithful attendance at the services the church provides for us. In the end, this makes it all the easier for us to fulfill our job of becoming vessels of love.

> *God loves us more than a father, mother, friend, or anyone else could love, and even more than we are able to love ourselves.*
>
> —St. John Chrysostom

We set ourselves on a path to become Christlike when we are living the life of the Church. God is love. To become like God, we need to experience God, and through the services, we come to do just that. This complements our acts of living the life of the Church by opening ourselves to the ascetical practices the tradition has to offer.

Training Tool

In the box on the next page, indicate what tends to hold you back from attending services in addition to the Sunday Divine Liturgy. What is one thing you can do to make it to another service?

SECTION 10

Get Over Yourself

St. Maximos the Confessor teaches us, "Cleanse your mind from anger, remembrance of evil, and shameful thoughts, and then you will find out how Christ dwells in you."

In one way or another, we can all relate to this teaching. I know I do. The decisions I've made that unintentionally hurt others, the feeding of my ego that again hurt others (and myself for that matter), the judgments I pass, the falling into the same unwanted behavior over and over—these and other concerns create a deep hurt in me and in others. Even though I know staying in this place of guilt does nothing good, I tend to get stuck. An unhealthy form of guilt is a way we choose to isolate ourselves from God, creating stress in our lives.

A healthy guilt or a feeling of shame for an action done is helpful, and we are granted this feeling to turn us to a fundamental change in our actions and thoughts. Then with a humble and contrite heart, we seek God's mercy.

In our hearts we remember everything He has done for us to take away these hurtful actions—dying for us so that we might be restored to our true nature. We are never beyond the scope of God's mercy. When we feel this and want to work on returning home, Saint Paul teaches us that there is nothing that can keep us from the love of God.

This refers us back to the concept of repentance, metanoia, that we discussed earlier. This act of repentance in the Orthodox Tradition is understood as a therapeutic approach. We have sinned, which is an action we do in which we choose to distance ourselves from God. However, we know that our true destiny is to be in union with God. Through sincere repentance we are able to be restored to God, and this is all He desires. We choose to put a plan in place to move ourselves away from the actions that led us into the sin or passion and back onto a path that leads us toward aligning ourselves with God's will.

Let us use our feelings of guilt in a healthy way. If we have fallen short (rather, *when* we fall short), let us allow that feeling of guilt to turn us to true metanoia. Guilt is no good unless it causes us to change for the better.

I recall a time when I was suffering greatly from a passion I fell into. I fell, and it hurt. It hurt others and myself. It was just painful all around. I felt such shame and guilt about the situation that I was blinded to the fact that I was not even truly repenting.

I was feeling more of the prideful feeling of "poor me, poor me." Pride is a two-sided coin—one side says "I am so great," and the other says "poor me." On either side, it is all about me. I kept thinking, "Poor Rita, what an idiot you are! How could you have done such a thing?" I could not let it go. I could not forgive myself and instead continued to hold onto feelings of guilt and shame.

Then, thank God, I was divinely put in the right place at the right time. I attended a retreat and heard a spiritual mother say something that has affected me to this day. She proposed the question, "Do we think we are better than God?"

That made me think: Better than God? Who on earth would think such a thing. Then she followed up her thought-provoking question with the comment, "If God can forgive us, then why can't we forgive ourselves?" She added, "Unless we are somehow better than God, then we must learn how to properly forgive not only others, but ourselves."

Humbled? That's exactly how I felt when I heard this. At that moment I realized I was in need of the therapy of true repentance. I had been thinking I was better than God, for I did not trust in God's mercy; I was stuck in my ego.

The Holy Fathers teach us that pride is the sin that is the cream of the crop. When we think God can't forgive us, that is a form of pride. The "poor me" card is a form of pride. We need to get over ourselves and trust that God forgives. When we don't accept that, we are essentially saying we know more than God. We know some greater reason God shouldn't or won't forgive us.

Because I was struggling with pride, I needed to make a plan not to fall into the passion again; and at the same time, I had to stop beating myself up for the fact that I had fallen. I fell, and I fell hard, yet through grace, God was there wanting to lift me back up.

I thought I was working on healthy repentance, but I came to realize the true purpose of guilt is only to drive you to humble repentance. Guilt is not there to make us feel bad and horrible about ourselves in the long term. It is a feeling we experience to drive us to our true needs, be it a change of heart, a change of thought, or a change of action.

> *Nothing so furthers teaching as this: loving and being loved.*
>
> —SAINT JOHN CHRYSOSTOM

Healthy guilt is a tool to drive us back home to our heavenly Father. We come crawling. We come sorrowful. We come knowing we are in need of healing. We come with tears, but these are tears of joyful sorrow, because we know when we want to turn away from our passions and work toward being with God, He always welcomes us with open arms. God is love. We will always be loved. Through repentance, He shows us the way to theosis and constantly partaking in Him.

It is the work of the evil one to make us feel we can never be forgiven. It is a tool of the evil one to continually remind us we are going to fall into the same sin (and unfortunately this does happen). However, grace covers all, and God is love. Love forgives. God forgives.

Unhealthy guilt is a form of stress on the body and soul. We need to practice self-forgiveness. Better yet, we need to practice true self-forgiveness—it goes hand in hand with working with God to put a plan in place to help us avoid giving in to the passion we fell into again.

I recall attempting to learn how to surf; I saw this experience as a spiritual teacher. First, the vast ocean makes you feel so small; yet at the same time when I am in the ocean (one of my favorite places to be), I feel surrounded by God's love. I feel it's the playground He gives to all creatures great and small (kids and adults alike).

Anyway, I would get knocked off my board (I still get knocked off my board), but then I'd get back on the board as fast as I possibly could. This is how it is when we fall. How fast do we pull ourselves back up to get back on track? Saint Augustine once said, "The church is not a hotel for saints, it is a hospital for sinners."

We are all sinners, but we have to rise above that. We need to get back on the board (on track) using the gifts tradition has taught us. This is a way for us to care for body and soul and to return us to our true nature.

I know I have spent a lot of time on this, but in my field of work I do see people harboring a lot of guilt when it comes to their eating and health practices. This book is meant to help us gain control in the areas of health that can foster our walk on the divine path.

Forgive and Love Others

Saint Maximos the Confessor teaches us:

> If you are remembering evil against someone, then pray for him; and as you remove through prayer the pain of the remembrance of the evil he has done, you will stop the advance of the passion. And when you have attained brotherly love and love for mankind, you will completely cast this passion out of your soul. Then when someone else does evil to you, be affectionate and humble toward him, and treat him kindly, and you will deliver him from this passion.

I really saw this teaching come alive when a woman I knew was struggling with anger toward her ex-husband. She suffered a great deal from the divorce and would speak with her spiritual father about the anger she felt toward

> *To bear a grudge and pray, means to sow seed on the sea and expect a harvest.*
> —Saint Isaac the Syrian

her ex. Her spiritual father kept telling her to pray for him.

She was not ready to hear this wisdom and would get so frustrated with what she was being told to do. Finally she started to faithfully pray for her ex, and when she truly prayed for him, this is when she began to feel better. It was quite easy to see the transformation taking place in her when she started this faithful process.

Praying for others is a gift we give to them in secret. (That is to say, they don't know we're praying for them.) Whether we are praying for friends or enemies, people near and dear or those we have never met, when we pray we are sharing with them a form of love; and yet they may have no clue we are doing so. Here are a few questions we could ask:

» Is there a co-worker that makes you fume? Pray for him.
» Is there a family member you want to shake? Pray for her.
» Is there a parishioner who gets under your skin? Pray for him.

Take some time to commit sincerely to praying for your enemies. Make a strong effort to pray for the person who has the amazing ability, as the expression goes, to ruffle your feathers, or (if his or her abilities are off the charts) to make you fit to be tied.

My dad always explains to me, "Rita, when we choose to be angry and not forgive someone, it's like we're choosing to put a chain around that person's neck and yank on it again and again, dragging that person with us wherever we go."

We must let go and practice loving forgiveness. Let's give this a try as a stress reliever. Whenever we start to feel anger toward others, let's try to instantly pray for them.

Training Tool

In the box below, list an area in your life where you feel some unhealthy guilt may be dwelling.

SECTION 11

Smile as You Simplify

Clean House

St. Basil the Great teaches us:

> The bread you do not use is the bread of the hungry. The garment hanging in your wardrobe is the garment of the person who is naked. The shoes you do not wear

> are the shoes of the one who is barefoot. The money you keep locked away is the money of the poor. The acts of charity you do not perform are the injustices you commit.

As we discussed earlier in this book, clutter can have an effect on our mental health and add to our stress. A great practice to incorporate into our lives is when we get something new, give something away. It's like our checks-and-balances system.

Another thing we can do is to do at least two major cleanings a year. Many people choose to do one of these during the Great Lent (Easter) fast, and the other can take place during the Nativity (Christmas) fast. This is another way to prevent the clutter from building up. If we have not used something for one year, this may be a good indicator it needs to be moved out of the house. It is a way to share what we are not using with someone in need.

We may also want to encourage this house cleaning within our church community. We should encourage everyone to do a house cleaning. The items gathered could then be donated to a thrift store or safe-home shelter.

Another option would be to hold a church rummage sale with the items parishioners are removing from their homes. The money raised at the rummage sale could be donated to a charity. As the saying goes, "One man's trash is another man's treasure."

Training Tool

In the box below, make a plan for a major house sweep. What rooms or closets will you tackle on what day? What types of items can you let go of?

Don't Overcommit

I'm one that wants to do everything. Let's go play bocce ball, sure; potluck—even better! I've come to realize that I bring chaos into my life when I overcommit, even when the activities are simply a matter of having a good time.

Now, when someone asks me to do something, I pause and respond, "Sounds great, let me check my schedule and get back to you." This one line has helped a lot. I used to immediately blurt out "Sure!" and before I knew it, I was committed to three dinner outings, two nutrition classes, and a partridge in a pear tree.

When we don't overcommit, we give ourselves more time to pray, give alms, and attend services. It is a way for us to keep balance in our days. It also gives us time to do more cooking.

SECTION 12

Cooking as a Destressor rather than a Stressor

I hear it from so many people all the time: "I don't have time to cook." Many times this simply has to do with the fact that we are overcommitted. The current reality cannot be denied: We are living very busy lives.

But another reality is that cooking and eating in the home, more often than not, make for a great way to care for health. Included in this section are some strategies for us to get a quick, nutritious, and delicious meal on the table with limited time.

Eating well is a way to care for body and soul. For one, it removes the physical stressor of not eating well; two, eating—as we have maintained throughout this book—is always a time to commune with the Divine.

It's time to get creative in the kitchen. Simply wearing an apron can change the whole feel of what is going on. Yes, it serves a practical purpose, but at the same time, it can symbolize the art of cooking.

Cooking can be a creative outlet versus just another daily task. Personally, I'd much rather cook dinner than fold laundry. To put it differently, I enjoy eating a tasty meal more than putting on a clean shirt.

Tips for Getting a Healthy Meal on the Table When Time Is Limited

1. *Cooking can be a family activity*

» When possible, assign other family members jobs. For example, one is in charge of slicing the tomatoes and prepping the lettuce. Before you know it, part of the salad is done. The sooner you can get your kids in the kitchen helping out, the better; by helping you, the kids will be developing skills for a lifetime.

- Have everyone in the family pick a meal for the week. Base your grocery list on this weekly menu. Many times the cooks of the household tell me, "It's not the cooking I have an issue with; it's deciding what to make."
- Divide and conquer: Do you get home later than everyone else? Assign those who arrive home before you some tasks to do. When you get home you find that the onions, broccoli, zucchini, and garlic have been chopped. Now your job is to sauté them while the pasta boils. You get home and feel you're on a cooking show.

2. Cook in stages

- Using onions and tomatoes in tonight's meal? Before you head to work, or the night before, just get these two items chopped. Then when you return home after work, having part of the meal prepped makes it seem like less of an overwhelming process. You come home and throw on that apron and feel like you're on a cooking show as you handle your prepped ingredients.
- Baking? Mix the dry ingredients ahead of time, then add the wet ones right before baking time.
- Grate cheese before you take the kids to soccer or head to your book club.

3. Celebrate cooking

» Pick a block of time available to you. Put on some music, throw on that fun apron, and plan on cooking the Saturday or Sunday afternoon away. Make some items in bulk. Many sauces, soups, casseroles, and quick breads freeze well. Freeze in meal-size portions.

» Find a cooking buddy. Plan that you will cook a soup and give them half the amount, and they do the same. You each save the other one cooking day.

» If you live alone, find a friend that you feed one night, and he or she feeds you the next.

» Take advantage of cooking gadgets such as the slow cooker and pressure cooker. The slow cooker is your personal chef while you're away at work, and the pressure cooker can cut cooking times down to less than half of what the stove-top time would be.

Please refer to Appendix III for a list of quick meal ideas.

Training Tool

In the box below, write what you will try to do to make sure more meals are being consumed in the home prepared from natural ingredients.

SECTION 13

Hobby Time

What is a hobby you enjoy? Taking time to practice a hobby is a wonderful way to destress, and it's time to make an appointment with ourselves.

To practice a hobby, we need to make sure we are not overcommitted in other areas of life. Making an appointment with ourselves is in itself a discipline.

When possible, allow this hobby to be something you can use to serve others, too. Here are a few examples:

» Enjoy knitting? Make a blanket as a baby gift or for someone in a nursing home.

» Like drawing or coloring? Make a card and send some fun mail. When was the last time you had a crayon in your hand?

» Enjoy photography? Take pictures, frame some, and donate them to a nursing home or shelter. Your hobby can add beauty to the world.

- Like making jewelry? Make some to be sold at a fundraiser or simply as a thinking-of-you gift.
- Enjoy fishing? Catch a fish and share it with some friends.
- Like gardening? Donate extra produce to a soup kitchen or surprise a neighbor with a bag.
- Enjoy hiking or beach time? Take some rubbish bags with you and pick up the trash that does not belong on the trail or beach.

Training Tool

In the box below, indicate what hobby you will take time to practice next. Set an appointment with yourself and make it happen.

Being under stress is something we all experience throughout our lives. I hope this stress section of the book didn't stress you out too much, and that you are closing this chapter with some practical faith-based tools to use in the future.

After attending a "Food, Faith, and Fasting" workshop, Matthew shares: "The importance of learning about a healthy relationship to a fitness regime caused me to have less stress in my life. It's okay to not feel like working out for a day, but I need to adjust my calorie intake, aiding me in not overeating and making more foods with real ingredients in the home versus eating out. This has also helped me financially. As a result of these changes, I feel better physically and mentally, and I've lost 10 pounds!"

CONCLUSION

And Now, Let the Journey Begin

Can one really write a conclusion for a topic that never ends? As a registered dietitian, I advise my clients to move away from diets, for they are temporary fads and fixes, and to embrace a lifestyle. That's a lifelong fix.

Together, through this book, we have learned practices that we can integrate into and use throughout our life. God willing, our faith is always going to be with us, and for the rest of our days, we will need to tend to our soul *and* to our body. We will always need to care for our health.

As we continue through our days, we're never going to be free from the cunning darts that the evil one throws our way, so let's continue to practice nepsis when it comes to our thoughts and feelings—and also to our health and eating practices.

Whether we are approaching eating, fasting, exercise, or

stress, handling these aspects of health in the proper spirit is of utmost importance. We must always remember the words of our Lord: "But seek first the kingdom of God and His righteousness, and all these things shall be added to you" (Matt. 6:33). When we put God first, things happen the way they are supposed to happen.

Cultivating and nurturing a care for both body and soul is an ongoing process. With the help of God, and as a support for one another, we can move toward allowing caring for our health to be a way to deepen our faith.

It has been a blessing for me to have this time with you. And may God grant you all many happy, healthy years!

APPENDIX I

Suggested Resources

Books

Clower, Will. *Eat Chocolate, Lose Weight*. Emmaus, PA: Rodale Books, 2014.

______ *The Fat Fallacy*. New York: Harmony Books, 2003.

_______ *The French Don't Diet Plan*. New York: Crown Publishers, 2006.

Coniaris, Anthony. *Daily Vitamins for Spiritual Growth*. Edina, MN: Light & Life Publishing, 2011.

Kessler, David. *The End of Overeating*. Emmaus, PA: Rodale Books, 2010.

Mosley, Michael and Spencer, Mimi. *The Fast Diet*. New York: Atria Books, 2015.

Pollan, Michael. *In Defense of Food: An Eater's Manifesto*. New York: Penguin Books, 2009.

Spidlik, Tomas. *Drinking from the Hidden Fountain, A Patristic Breviary: Ancient Wisdom for Today's World*. Kalamazoo, MI: Cistercian Publications, 1993.

Wansink, Brian. *Mindless Eating*. New York: Bantam, 2010.

Websites

This website offers weight loss and chronic disease prevention/ management programs: http://www.willclower.com

Podcasts on food and the Ancient Christian Faith: http://www.ancientfaith.com/podcasts/foodfaithfasting

Magazine Article: "Eating in an Anciently Refreshing Way" http://www.antiochian.org/node/25372

One-hour documentary on intermittent fasting: *Eat, Fast and Live Longer*: http://www.dailymotion.com/video/xvdbtt_eat-fast-live-longer-hd_shortfilms

One-hour documentary on short bursts of exercise: *The Truth about Exercise*: http://vimeo.com/51836895

7-minute exercise workout (A website with a full body workout in 7 minutes): http://www.7-min.com/

Christian-based health coaching and the book, *The Holistic Christian Woman*, are available at: http://www.theholistic-christianwoman.com/

Smartphone Exercise Apps

Sworkit (Great app for short bursts of exercise)

7-minute workout (An app that provides a full body workout in 7 minutes)

APPENDIX II

Recipes

RECIPES WITHOUT ANIMAL PRODUCTS

Here are some recipes that are free of animal products. Many of these recipes can have dairy and meat incorporated into them for non-fasting days; suggestions are given for doing this.

Angel Hair with Vegetables

Serves 4–6

Earthy Ingredients

» 8 ounces raw angel hair pasta
» 3 tablespoons olive oil
» 1 cup chopped tomato
» 3½ cups chopped broccoli (stems and florets)
» 2 cloves garlic, finely minced
» 1 tablespoon fresh basil or 1 teaspoon dried (optional)
» Salt and fresh ground pepper to taste

Delectable Directions

- Steam broccoli until tender.
- Bring 8 cups of water to a rapid boil. Cook pasta in boiling water.
- Place 1 tablespoon of olive oil in a skillet, and on low heat sauté garlic until fragrant.
- Then add in tomato. Sauté until tomatoes are softened.
- Then add in broccoli.
- Once pasta is cooked and drained, add to veggie mixture and add in rest of olive oil, basil, and salt and pepper to taste. Serve warm or cold.

Become an Artist of the Kitchen

- Switch up the vegetables.
- Add some cooked shrimp.
- Add some canned salmon.
- Add in some crumbled Italian sausage.
- Use whole wheat angel hair pasta.
- Add some pine nuts for extra protein and omega-3 fatty acids.
- Use other herbs of choice.
- Top with some freshly grated parmesan cheese.

Easy Black Bean Salsa

Serves 6–16

(depending on whether used as a dip or an entrée)

This recipe can be prepared in a short time. You can use it as an appetizer, side dish, or the main entree.

Earthy Ingredients

- 1½ cups cooked black beans (canned or prepared from the dried state)
- 1½ cups cooked corn (canned or freshly cooked)
- 1½ cups salsa
- ¼ cup cilantro, chopped
- 1½ tablespoons fresh lime juice

Delectable Directions

- Mix all of the above together and use this as your base.
- Serve on top of a salad, in a wrap, on top of a baked potato, or on top of corn chips for a taco salad.

Become an Artist of the Kitchen

- Add some chopped vegetables or fruit such as bell pepper, carrot, yellow onion, green onion, avocado, tomato, mango, or pineapple.
- Top the salsa with grilled veggies.
- Add a chopped chili or jalapeño for a spicy flavor. Or add some chili powder.

It is important to make sure you are consuming a food that contains vitamin C when you eat a plant-based source of iron. This helps your body to absorb the iron found in the plant-based food. For example, beans are a great source of iron. But for your body to absorb the iron from the beans, a vitamin C food source must be consumed at the same meal. So enjoy beans with tomatoes or have some pineapple as a side dish. It works well to include lemon or lime juice as part of a bean recipe.

Marinated Mushrooms

Serves 8–12 as an appetizer

Earthy Ingredients

- » 1 pound fresh mushrooms
- » ¼ cup lemon juice
- » ½ cup olive oil
- » 2 green onions with tops, thinly sliced
- » ¼ cup fresh parsley, chopped
- » 1 clove garlic, finely chopped
- » ¾ teaspoon salt
- » ¼ teaspoon freshly ground pepper

Delectable Directions

- » Cut mushrooms into 1/8-inch slices.
- » Mix mushroom slices and lemon juice in large glass bowl.
- » Stir in oil, onions, ¼ cup parsley, garlic, salt, pepper.
- » Toss, cover, and refrigerate at least 3 hours, stirring occasionally.
- » Serve with a slotted spoon.

Become an Artist of the Kitchen

- » Garnish with paprika. It adds nice color and flavor.
- » Garnish with parsley sprigs.
- » Try a mixture of a variety of different mushrooms.
- » Add an additional clove of garlic.

Korean Green Beans

Serves 10–14

Earthy Ingredients

- » 2 pounds green beans, stems removed
- » 3 tablespoons sesame oil
- » 1 tablespoon rice vinegar
- » 1 teaspoon sugar
- » 1 tablespoon lemon juice
- » 1 teaspoon fresh grated ginger
- » 2 tablespoons sesame seeds
- » ¼ teaspoon kosher salt

Delectable Directions

- » Bring a large pot of water to a boil.
- » Add the green beans and cook, uncovered, until crisp-tender, 3 to 4 minutes. Drain and set aside.
- » In a large bowl, whisk together the remaining ingredients until well blended.
- » Add the green beans and toss to combine well.

Become an Artist of the Kitchen

- » Try this base with another veggie of choice.
- » Leave out the sesame seeds.
- » Use honey instead of sugar.

Lentils with Kale Soup

Serves 4–6

Earthy Ingredients

» 1 cup lentils

» 8 cups water

» 1 large potato, diced

» ½ bunch Swiss chard or kale, coarsely chopped

» 1 medium onion, coarsely chopped

» Salt and pepper to taste

» 3 tablespoons olive oil

» Lemon wedges

Delectable Directions

» Wash lentils, add water, cover, and cook until almost tender.

» Heat olive oil in a skillet on low-medium, sauté onions, then add salt and pepper.

» Add the diced potatoes to the lentils; boil for 10 minutes. Add more water if necessary.

» Add Swiss chard or kale to lentil mixture and cook until all vegetables are done, no more than 10 minutes. Serve with lemon wedges.

Become an Artist of the Kitchen

» Use spinach instead of kale. Or use a variety of greens.

» Try different types of onions.

Moroccan Style Chick Peas

Serves 4–6

Earthy Ingredients

- 1 15-ounce can garbanzo beans (or ~1½ cups cooked from the dried state)
- 2 tablespoons olive oil
- ¼ teaspoon chili powder
- 1 teaspoon cumin
- ½ teaspoon salt
- 1 tablespoon lemon juice

Delectable Directions

- In a small pot, on low-medium heat, heat olive oil.
- Add chili powder and cumin and cook for a minute to release flavor.
- Add all other ingredients and heat through.
- Serve over rice, with pita, or simply by itself.

Become an Artist of the Kitchen

- Sauté a bit of onion with the spices.
- Top with some fresh cilantro.
- Add in some chopped tomato.

Balsamic Vinaigrette Salad Dressing

Serves 2–4

Earthy Ingredients

- 3 tablespoons olive oil
- 1 tablespoon balsamic vinegar
- Brown mustard to reach a consistency you like

Delectable Directions

- Mix all the ingredients together.

Become an Artist of the Kitchen

- Add herbs or spices (oregano, basil, garlic, cayenne, etc.).
- You may want to add a tad bit of honey.
- Try a different type of vinegar, such as white wine vinegar.

This salad dressing is a great gift idea. Think of placing it in a unique bottle or have the kids creatively decorate the bottle.

Tip

Make a larger quantity and store in the refrigerator. Take out, let come to room temperature, and mix before using.

Beans and Greens

Serves 4–6

Earthy Ingredients

» 4 large garlic cloves, thinly sliced

» 3 tablespoons extra virgin olive oil

» Pinch of red pepper flakes

» 1 can or 1½ cups cooked cannellini beans (reserving ⅓ cup liquid)

» 1½ pounds of chopped kale

» Salt and pepper to taste

Delectable Directions

» In a medium pot, sauté sliced garlic and red pepper flakes in oil on low-medium heat until aroma is released.

» Add the chopped kale and sauté until completely wilted.

» Add beans and simmer until heated through but still firm.

» Add salt and pepper to taste.

» Place in bowls. Drizzle a little extra virgin olive oil on the top of each bowl.

» Serve with a nice piece of crusty bread or simply by itself.

Become an Artist of the Kitchen

» Top with parmesan cheese.

» Top with crumbled hot Italian sausage.

» For a soupier dish, add a bit of water or more bean juice.

Simply Teriyaki Sauce

Makes about 2 cups

Earthy Ingredients

» 1 cup brown sugar (or less)

» 1 cup soy sauce

» 1 cup Mirin (rice cooking wine)

Delectable Directions

» Over medium heat, bring all ingredients to a boil.

» Stir till sugar dissolves.

» Reduce heat and gently simmer, stirring occasionally, until slightly thickened.

» Let cool.

Notes

» If you would like a slightly thicker sauce, add some corn or potato starch while mixture is on simmer.

» Will keep in fridge for 1–2 months. So make extra to store.

» This sauce has a strong flavor, so a little will go a long way. Add to stir-fries or use as a marinade.

Become an Artist of the Kitchen

» Use some honey instead of all brown sugar.

» Try on a variety of different steamed veggies.

FASTING DESSERTS

Baked Pears with Chocolate

Serves 4–8

Earthy Ingredients

» 4 Bosc pears (sliced in half lengthwise, cores removed)

» 1 cup apple juice

» 8 teaspoons dark chocolate chips

Delectable Directions

» Place pears in baking dish, cut side up.

» Pour apple juice evenly over pears.

» Fill each pear half with 1 teaspoon of chocolate chips.

» Bake for approximately 40 to 45 minutes or until soft.

Become an Artist of the Kitchen

» Instead of filling pears with chocolate, try some chopped walnuts or other nuts of choice.

» Top pears with a dash of cinnamon.

» Substitute apples for pears.

» Add less chocolate to pears.

Dark chocolate is our friend! It contains flavonoids, which are naturally occurring compounds found in plants that have many health benefits, such as antioxidant qualities.

This antioxidant quality helps to limit damage that can be caused to cells in our body. These flavonoids have also been shown to help with the prevention of cardiovascular disease and to help control high levels of LDL or "bad" cholesterol. Remember, the darker the better (try for at least 70% cocoa), and portion control is key. A hint to help with portion control is when you eat dark chocolate, don't use your teeth. Let it just slowly melt away in your mouth.

Orange Cake

Serves 12–16

Earthy Ingredients

- 1½ cups all-purpose flour
- ½ cup sugar
- 1 teaspoon baking soda
- ½ teaspoon baking powder
- ½ teaspoon salt
- 1 cup orange juice
- ¼ cup coconut oil
- 1 tablespoon orange zest (grated orange peel)
- 1 tablespoon white vinegar
- 1½ teaspoons vanilla

Delectable Directions

- Preheat oven to 350°.
- Grease and flour a Bundt pan or one 8" x 8" pan.
- Whisk together thoroughly: flour, sugar, baking soda, and salt. Add orange juice, coconut oil, orange zest, vinegar, and vanilla. Stir together until smooth.
- Scrape the batter into the pan and spread evenly. Bake for approximately 30 to 35 minutes or until a toothpick inserted into the center comes out clean.
- Let cool in the pan on a rack for 10 minutes. Slide a thin knife around the cake to detach it from the pan. Invert the cake. Let cool right side up on a rack.

Become an Artist of the Kitchen

» Use lemon zest instead of orange zest.

» Use pineapple juice instead of orange juice.

» Decorate the cake with powdered sugar and/or fruit slices of choice and some mint.

No-Bake Chocolate Macaroons

Makes 20 plus (Remember, a little goes a long way, so the smaller you make them the better.)

Earthy Ingredients

- 1½ cups plus 2 tablespoons unsweetened coconut flakes
- ¼ teaspoon vanilla
- ¾ cup raw cocoa powder
- ½ cup maple syrup
- 1 tablespoon coconut oil
- A pinch of sea salt

Delectable Directions

- In a large bowl, place coconut, add vanilla, and mix.
- Add all other ingredients and stir well.
- Roll batter into ¾-inch balls and place on tray that can be frozen (batter will be wet, so expect to get your hands messy).
- Leave tray in freezer for 30 minutes to set.
- Remove from freezer and transfer balls to an airtight container.
- Store in refrigerator until serving.

Become an Artist of the Kitchen

- Replace the vanilla with 1 tablespoon of dark rum or a different liquor of choice.

Peanut Butter Cups

Makes 8 in regular-size muffin tin or 16 mini

Earthy Ingredients

- ½ cup dark chocolate chips
- 8 teaspoons peanut butter

Delectable Directions

- On a stove top in a double broiler, melt the chocolate.
- Place approximately 2 teaspoons of melted chocolate in the bottom of each muffin cup.
- You do not have to be exact, but at least make sure the chocolate covers the bottom of the muffin cup. Make sure you do not make the layer too thick, because you will need enough chocolate to cover the top.
- Now freeze the muffin tin until chocolate hardens—about 5 to 7 minutes.
- Remove tray from freezer. Spread 1 teaspoon of peanut butter over hardened chocolate in each cup. Gently smooth out, trying not to get the peanut butter on the end of the muffin cups.
- Cover peanut butter with 2 tsp. chocolate. Freeze again.
- When hardened, pop peanut butter cups out of muffin tins and enjoy, or place in an airtight container and refrigerate.

Become an Artist of the Kitchen

- Add a pinch of sea salt.
- Try a different kind of nut butter.

Banana Cake

Serves 24–28

Earthy Ingredients

» 2 cups flour

» 4 ripe bananas, mashed

» 1 teaspoon baking soda

» 1 teaspoon baking powder

» 1/8 teaspoon salt

» 1/3 cup coconut oil

» ¾ cup brown sugar

» ¼ cup plus 1 tablespoon orange juice

» 1 teaspoon vanilla

» 1 cup walnuts, chopped

Delectable Directions

» Preheat oven to 350°.

» Mix flour, baking soda, baking powder, and salt.

» Add all other ingredients and mix until combined.

» Place in a greased Bundt pan or 9" x 13" pan.

» Bake for 40 minutes and test with a toothpick. Toothpick should come out clean.

Become an Artist of the Kitchen

» Replace the vanilla with 1 teaspoon of cinnamon.

» Use a different type of nut.

FISH RECIPES

Fish Souvlaki

Serves 4–6

Earthy Ingredients

» 2½ tablespoons fresh lemon juice

» 2½ teaspoons dried oregano

» ¼ cup olive oil

» ¾ teaspoon salt

» 6 garlic cloves, minced

» 1 pound white fish of choice, cut into 1-inch pieces

Delectable Directions

» Mix first 5 ingredients in a sealable container. Add fish pieces and coat all sides with marinade. Marinate in refrigerator for 30 minutes, turning once.

» Remove fish from marinade.

» Heat a pan coated lightly with some of the marinade over medium-high heat or grill (grill on skewers).

» Add fish and cook until fish is cooked through.

» Serve on pita bread with sliced tomato and lettuce.

Become an Artist of the Kitchen

» Serve fish on top of a salad.

» Try this recipe with shrimp instead of fish.

Mediterranean Tuna Salad

Serves 1–6 (depending on whether served as a meal or an appetizer)

Earthy Ingredients

- 5 ounces canned chunk light tuna, drained (fresh cooked tuna can also be used)
- 1 tablespoon red onion, finely diced
- 2 tablespoons chopped kalamata olives
- ½ tablespoon capers
- 1½ tablespoons olive oil
- 2 teaspoons Dijon mustard
- Salt and pepper

Delectable Directions

- Mix all together. Add salt and pepper to taste.
- Serve on toast, crackers, pita bread, crostini, or on top of a salad.

Become an Artist of the Kitchen

- Try different olives.
- Add chopped marinated artichokes.
- Add a chopped sundried tomato.
- If you have leftover fish, try using that instead of tuna.

REPLACEMENTS FOR SODAS

Mint Green Tea

Serves 8–12

Earthy Ingredients

- 8 cups water
- 6 green tea bags
- Approximately 1 to 1½ cups fresh mint leaves, slightly ripped (to help release flavor)
- 3 tablespoons of sugar (Decrease by ½ tablespoon each time you make it.)

Delectable Directions

- In a large pot, bring water to a boil. Remove from heat and mix in sugar until dissolved. Add the mint and tea bags and steep for approximately 10 minutes.
- Remove tea bags and let cool. Once cooled, strain out mint leaves and store in a container. Place in fridge.
- Let chill for several hours. Serve over ice.

Become an Artist of the Kitchen

- Try using black tea.
- Add a splash of lemon.
- Use honey instead of sugar.
- Garnish glass with mint leaves.
- Mix tea with pineapple juice instead of using sugar.

Grape or Pineapple Spritzers

Serves 1–2

Earthy Ingredients

» ½ cup grape or pineapple juice

» ½ cup seltzer water

» ¾ teaspoon lime (optional)

Delectable Directions

» Mix all ingredients together.

Become an Artist in the Kitchen

» Try this with a different fruit juice.

» Add some fresh muddled mint.

» Add a splash of lemon instead of lime.

NOTE: At first you may notice you need to start with a higher juice-to-water ratio, but over time, as you decrease the sugar in your overall diet, you will realize that your juice-to-water ratio will be similar to the one the recipe above suggests.

NON-FASTING MEALS & MORE

Some of these recipes have suggestions for ways they can be altered to be fast-appropriate.

Good (and Easy) Granola

Makes about 4 cups

Earthy Ingredients

- » 4 cups oats (use quick oats for a granola bar with a softer consistency or old-fashioned oats for granola with a harder consistency)
- » ½ cup softened butter or 7 tablespoons coconut oil
- » ½ cup brown sugar (or less)
- » ¼ cup to ⅓ cup chopped nuts of choice

Delectable Directions

- » Preheat oven to 350°. Grease a 9" x 13" baking pan.
- » Mix all the above ingredients together. Place mixture in greased baking pan. Bake for 23 to 25 minutes or until lightly browned. Let sit and slightly cool.
- » Roughly cut into chunks or crumble into loose granola.
- » Store the granola in an airtight container.
- » This recipe serves as a very versatile base.

Become an Artist of the Kitchen

» Add some ground flax seed, sunflower seeds, raisins, dried fruit, or shredded coconut.

» Add some cinnamon or a teaspoon of vanilla. Or you could add a tiny bit of maple syrup or honey.

» When adding some other form of food that could sweeten the granola, hold back a bit on the amount of brown sugar.

» You could also add ½ cup to ¾ cup of nut butter and leave out the chopped nuts.

Ramen Noodle Soup

Serves 6–8

Earthy Ingredients

- » 1 (8-ounce) package dried ramen, somen noodles, or angel hair
- » 4 cups chicken broth (low-sodium)
- » 2 cups water
- » 3 garlic cloves, chopped
- » 2 tablespoons fresh ginger
- » 2 to 3 tablespoons soy sauce (use just enough for flavoring)
- » 1 teaspoon sugar
- » Toppings (see suggestions below)

Delectable Directions

- » Cook noodles of choice following directions on package. Rinse with cold water and set aside.
- » In a large pot over medium-high heat, add chicken broth, water, sugar, and ginger; bring just to a boil. Reduce heat to low. Add soy sauce and your favorite vegetable toppings; simmer for 5 minutes longer or until toppings are almost cooked.
- » Increase heat to medium, stir in noodles, and cook for approximately 4 to 6 minutes.
- » Place cooked noodles in a large soup bowl; spoon broth mixture (with toppings) over the top and serve.

Become an Artist of the Kitchen

» To keep this recipe fast-appropriate, use vegetable broth and select fasting additions.

» Soups are all about the broth. When in the "cooking artist" mode, experiment with creating your own broth or stock.

Add in your favorites and come up with some others too:

Vegetable Toppings	**Additional Toppings**
Sliced carrots	Baked ham slices
Sliced celery	Roast pork slices
Sliced green cabbage	Cooked shrimp
Chopped bok choy	Egg
Sliced mushroom	Fish cake
Green peas	Hot sauce
Sliced sweet onion	Fish sauce
Sliced green onions	Lime juice
Sliced daikon	Lemon juice
Sprouts	Kimchi
Sliced tomato	Rice vinegar
Choy Sum	Miso paste

Sausage Patties

Makes 8–10

Earthy Ingredients

» 1 pound ground pork

» ¼ cup water

» 1–2 cloves minced garlic

» ¾ teaspoon thyme

» ¾ teaspoon fennel seeds

» ½ teaspoon salt

» Cooking oil

Delectable Directions

» In a bowl, combine pork, garlic, thyme, fennel seeds, and salt; mix until just combined.

» Cover and refrigerate up to 24 hours.

» Shape mixture into patties.

» Lightly coat skillet with cooking oil.

» Place skillet over moderate heat until hot.

» Add patties to skillet.

» Cook about 7 minutes on each side or until browned.

Become an Artist of the Kitchen

» Note: You can use other spices of choice such as crushed red pepper, allspice, garlic powder, cayenne, paprika.

For a Portuguese-flavored sausage, substitute the ingredients below for the thyme and fennel seeds. Keep the garlic and salt.

- » 1–2 chili peppers, chopped
- » ¼ teaspoon cayenne
- » ¼ –⅓ teaspoon paprika
- » ¼ teaspoon black pepper
- » ¼ teaspoon cinnamon
- » ¼ teaspoon coriander
- » ½ tablespoon vinegar

Macaroni and Cheese

Serves 14–16

Earthy Ingredients

» ¼ cup butter (and some to grease baking dish)

» ¼ cup all-purpose flour

» 3 cups whole milk

» 2¾ teaspoons salt

» 1 pound elbow macaroni

» 2 cups shredded cheddar cheese (or extra sharp cheddar)

» 3 cups water

Delectable Directions

» Preheat oven to 400°.

» Butter 13" x 9" x 2" baking dish.

» Melt ¼ cup butter in a large saucepan over medium-high heat. Add flour; cook, whisking constantly, for 1 minute.

» Whisk in milk and water. Bring to a boil, reduce heat to a simmer, and cook, whisking often to make sure no clumps are present, approximately 10 minutes.

» Stir in salt. Remove sauce from heat, add in pasta and cheese, and stir till cheese is melted.

» Add mixture to baking dish, making sure all the noodles are covered in sauce. Then cover with foil. Bake until pasta is tender, about 30 minutes.

Become an Artist of the Kitchen

- » In a small pan, toast some panko or other bread crumbs with some butter on low heat; sprinkle on top of macaroni and cheese before baking.
- » Try a different type of cheese.
- » Add some diced onion.
- » Add a dash of paprika.

APPENDIX III

Resource Guides

Some Fasting Tips

Examples of Substitutions

- Try coconut or almond milk in coffee, teas, cereals, or creamed soup recipes (coconut milk is a bit sweet so factor this quality into your cooking). As with any food, make sure the ingredients the product contains are real, and use in moderation.
- Make a pesto sauce, leaving out the cheese. (Pesto sauces freeze well.)
- For a dessert, try a piece of dark chocolate. (Dark chocolate that is at least 70% cocoa is beneficial to your health.)
- For protein sources, instead of meat, fish, and poultry, try beans, tempeh, nuts, and whole grains.

Fasting Breakfast Ideas

- Oatmeal with apple or banana slices, walnuts, cinnamon, and a tiny bit of maple syrup or brown sugar
- Apple or banana slices topped with a nut butter such as peanut or almond

- Bagel with avocado, tomato, and garlic powder
- Toast with peanut butter and honey or jam
- Granola with nuts, half a piece of fruit
- Trail mix
- Fruit smoothie made with coconut milk
- Make a mixture of tahini (sesame seed paste) and molasses. Eat on a slice of bread or on apple or banana slices.
- Figs or other dried fruit and walnuts

Fasting Lunches and Dinners

- Avocado and tomato sandwich, nuts, dark chocolate
- Taco salad: pinto beans, served over corn chips or a tortilla, topped with lettuce, salsa, and sautéed veggies
- Fried rice with vegetables, cashews, and pineapple
- Lentil soup, tomato and cucumber salad
- Coconut milk-based soup, salad, dark chocolate
- Olive tapenade bagel sandwich, fruit, dark chocolate-covered nuts
- Hummus, tomato, and mint sandwich, side of carrots and bell pepper, nuts
- Maki roll, soybeans, seaweed salad, tea
- Black bean soup, sweet potato, pineapple
- Roasted beets, sweet potatoes and carrots, salad
- Vegetable soup, bread, nuts, dark chocolate
- Tempeh, rice, vegetables
- Avocado topped with a mixture of wasabi and soy sauce, rice, sautéed veggies of choice

» Pasta tossed with sautéed veggies, pine nuts, side salad

» Seaweed paper wrap filled with rice, soybeans, and veggies of choice

» White bean soup, roasted broccoli, dark chocolate

» Baked potato or sweet potato topped with salsa and sautéed veggies of choice, dark chocolate-covered nuts

» Salad topped with balsamic vinaigrette, seeds of choice, garbanzo or kidney beans, avocado

Good Sources of Calcium (dairy-free)

Almonds	Macadamia nuts	Tahini
Bok Choy	Beans	Kale
Collard greens	Rhubarb	Brazil nuts
Watercress	Broccoli	Turnips
Figs	Spinach	Blackstrap molasses
Golden raisins		

Oil Substitutes for Oil-Free Fasts

» Various vinegars, soy sauce, a tiny bit of olive juice, vegetable broth, vegetable juice, or simply water mixed with hot sauce or herbs and spices can be used to replace oils when sautéing vegetables.

» The liquid remaining from cooking beans or vegetables can add flavor to a soup broth and can also be used as a sautéing base.

Yummy Yogurt!

Let's examine two different types of yogurt. One is a 6-ounce cup of yogurt that is low-fat with fruit on the bottom. It contains 29 grams of sugar and 190 calories per serving. The other is a plain full-fat yogurt that contains 9 grams of sugar and 130 calories per serving.

Believe it or not, the low-fat version contains more calories per serving. But counting calories should not be the main focus.

Choose foods that are made up of real ingredients, and then portion control will come through serving ourselves less and taking our time as we eat.

When choosing yogurt, the best choice is the plain full-fat kind (Greek or regular, your preference). Then have fun jazzing it up. It is always better to buy the plain version of yogurt, because then you have control over the amount of sweetener you add into it. The prepackaged flavored ones have already been loaded up with sugar for you. Using a small amount of sweetener is fine. But when something contains 10 teaspoons of sugar per serving, our caution flag should go up.

Yogurt for Breakfast, Anyone?

Start with plain full-fat yogurt and then add toppings to create a combination that is pleasing to you. Here are some suggestions in the chart below. You don't have to incorporate every row, so base it on what you are feeling that day. Basically, pick things from the various boxes and create a delightful yogurt that sounds good to you!

In bold below is an example of a great combination.

Fruit	Sweetener	Toppings	Flavorings
Berries of choice	The fruit or granola alone may add enough	Granola	Grated fresh ginger
Banana slices	Maple syrup	**Nuts**	Dash of vanilla
Apple slices	Honey	Cereal	**Pinch of cinnamon**
Pineapple chunks	**Brown sugar**	Dark chocolate chips	Pinch of cocoa powder
Dried fruit, finely chopped	Fruit juice	Ground flax seed	Dash of almond extract

Quick Meal Ideas

- When making sauces or dressings, make extra and keep in the fridge for a later use.
- Jazz up baked potatoes or sweet potatoes. Kids love a baked potato bar where they get to pick their toppings.
- Rice noodles take no time to cook and can be the base for many meals. Keep a package in the pantry. Remember

to use the sauces you already have made.

- Angel hair pasta and couscous can be staples in the pantry as they only take 3 to 5 minutes to cook in boiling water. Top them with sautéed veggies and some other fixings of choice, such as shrimp or chicken, and you're on your way to a meal.
- Extra rice? It's time for fried rice, and this can be a great way to eat more veggies.
- How about a tuna fish salad or sandwich with some fresh fruit on the side and some nuts.
- Fish can be cooked quickly and does not need to marinate for a long time.
- If you have leftover meat, cut it up before putting it away. Now you have one ingredient prepped for a meal you will have on another night.
- An omelet for dinner always works.
- Taco salads are quick, easy, and can be very nutritious. Open up a can of beans, top with lettuce, sour cream, diced peppers, salsa, and olives.
- Sub night: Buy some fresh bread, top with veggies, add some meat and/or cheese slices and vinaigrette; serve with nuts, salad, or fruit.
- Have a box or can of broth on hand at all times. Need a quick meal? Make a soup with some chopped veggies, noodles, and herbs.
- What about a toasted cheese sandwich topped with a tomato?
- Prepare unpeeled shrimp with a marinade. It will take less time and it will cause people to eat the shrimp slowly. Remember, eating slowly does help to control portion size.

» Make a batch of granola; it keeps for weeks.

» Make a large amount of a fruit smoothie and store the extra in the fridge.

» Fresh bread, fresh vegetables topped with a balsamic vinaigrette, olives, sliced cheese, and maybe some nuts.

» Hard-boiled egg, bread, sliced tomatoes.

» Sauté vegetables in olive oil, serve with bread and some slices of meat and/or cheese.

Substitutes for Highly Sweetened Drinks

- Add herbs or slices of fruit to your water (or create a combination).

Orange	Lemon	Peppermint	Apple
Lime	Pineapple	Spearmint	Tangerine
Cucumber	Pear	Ginger	Basil

- Mix ¾ cup sparkling mineral water (carbonated water) with ⅛ cup or less of 100% fruit juice of choice.
- Tea (can be made from the bag or purchased without sweetener)
  * Try a new tea. Many say they do not like tea, but there may be a tea they never tried that they would like.
  * Enjoy it iced or hot.
  * You can add a bit of honey or sugar. Just focus on using less. Gradually your taste for sugar will subside, and you will be satisfied with using less in your drink.
- Coffee
  * You can drink coffee black, or with some cream and/or sugar. Just be aware of the amount of cream and sugar you are adding. A little bit does go a long way.
- Coconut water
- Beer, wine, or liquor
- Lemonade made with real lemon and a bit of sugar
- Hot cocoa. Make it from scratch and use more cocoa and less sugar. Refrigerate it to create a chocolate milk.
- Fruit smoothie
- Simply a mug of warm water

Remember:

With calorie-laden beverages, it is all about the amount. Enjoy the beverage but just be aware of the amount you are having. Serve yourself in smaller cups, and serve yourself less than you usually would. Take your time with your beverage.

Whenever you make a beverage yourself, you control the amount of sugar that goes into it. But if you buy a beverage that contains sugar, it usually contains way more sugar than you would've put into it if you made it yourself.

As we hear over and over again, too much of anything can be harmful to us. So as with anything, this list of drinks should be used with balance and moderation.

How Can Sugar Fit into a Healthy Diet?

The World Health Organization has made a recommendation of no more than 6 teaspoons of added sweetener (24 grams) a day for overall health and weight management. (4 grams of sugar is equal to 1 teaspoon.)

Currently on a daily basis, Americans are eating on average close to 22 teaspoons of added sweetener. These come from table sugar, high-fructose corn syrup, honey, dextrose, and so forth.

Our goal is to always use the real deal (sugar, honey, etc.) but use less of it.

So how can this add up?

- 10 teaspoons of sugar (in the form of high-fructose corn syrup or sugar) in a can of Pepsi
- Approximately 3 to 5 added teaspoons of sugar in ¾-cup flavored yogurt. Examples:
    - 1 cup Chobani non-fat strawberry-flavored yogurt: 4¼ teaspoons sugar
    - 6 ounces Brown Cow maple-flavored yogurt: 3 added teaspoons sugar
- 1 cup of Honey Nut Cheerios: approximately 4 teaspoons sugar
- 1 packet of flavored instant oatmeal: approximately 3 teaspoons of added sugar
- 1 20-ounce bottle of SoBe green tea: 15¼ teaspoons

» Approximately 2½ to 3½ teaspoons sugar in ½ cup vanilla ice cream

» Approximately 1 teaspoon sugar in ½ tablespoon semi-sweet chocolate chips (approximately 50% cocoa)

» 8-ounce cup of black coffee: you add 1 teaspoon of sugar

Your goal is to avoid fake sweeteners. When having sweeteners, choose foods and beverages made with the real deal. Try to stay under 6 teaspoons of added sugar a day.

Check out the following examples of how easy it is to go over your sugar allotment for the day and, conversely, how easy it is to stay under.

Examples of Daily Sugar Intake

Food or Drink	**Sweetener per Serving**
12-ounce can Pepsi	10 teaspoons
	Over for the day

1 cup Honey Nut Cheerios	4 teaspoons
1 tsp. sugar in afternoon tea	1 teaspoon
12-ounce Gatorade	2 teaspoons
	Over for the day

6-oz prepackaged maple-flavored yogurt	3 teaspoons
8-oz Starbucks Chai Latte	4 teaspoons
	Over for the day

½ cup oatmeal with 1 tsp. brown sugar, apple pieces, walnuts for breakfast	1 teaspoon
1 teaspoon honey in afternoon tea	1 teaspoon
½ cup vanilla ice cream for dinner dessert	3 teaspoons
	Under for the day

1/3 cup plain yogurt with ½ teaspoon brown sugar, banana slices, pecans for breakfast	½ teaspoon
Coffee with sugar	½ teaspoon
½ tablespoon semisweet chocolate chips with some peanut butter after dinner	1 teaspoon
	Under for the day

4 oz full-fat plain yogurt with ¾ teaspoon brown sugar	¾ teaspoon
1 teaspoon honey in afternoon tea	1 teaspoon
1½" square of shortbread	1 teaspoon
	Under for the day

Fasting and Fast-free Seasons of the Orthodox Liturgical Calendar

As listed on www.oca.org. Slight variations in practice exist among various jurisdictions and parishes, so check with your priest for your local practice.

Fasting Seasons

» Nativity (St. Philip's Fast): Nov. 15–Dec. 24 (Nov. 28–Jan. 6 Old Calendar)

» Meatfast: Monday after the Sunday of Last Judgment through Cheesefare Sunday

» Great Lent & Holy Week: First Monday of Great Lent through Great and Holy Saturday

» Apostles' (Ss. Peter & Paul) Fast: Monday after All Saints' Sunday through June 28 (July 11 OC)

» Dormition (Theotokos) Fast: Aug. 1 –14 (Aug. 14–27 OC)

Fast-Free Weeks

» Afterfeast of the Nativity of Christ to Theophany Eve: Dec. 25–Jan. 4 (Jan. 7–17 OC)

» The week following the Sunday of the Publican & Pharisee: Second Week of the Lenten Triodion

» Bright Week: Pascha through St. Thomas Sunday

» Trinity Week: Pentecost through All Saints Sunday

Fast Days

- The Wednesdays and Fridays of the year, except for fast-free weeks
- The Eve of Theophany: January 5 (January 18 OC)
- The Beheading of St. John the Baptist: August 29 (September 11 OC)
- The Elevation of the Cross: September 14 (September 27 OC)

NOTES

1 Coniaris, Anthony. *Philokalia: The Bible of Orthodox Spirituality*. Light & Life Pub. Co., 1998, p. 100

2 Coniaris, *op. cit.*, p. 90

3 Coniaris, *op. cit.*, p. 91

4 http://lifehacker.com/how-clutter-affects-your-brain-and-what-you-can-do-abo-662647035 [accessed February 16, 2015]

5 Food additives and hyperactive behaviour in 3-year-old and 8/9-year-old children in the community: a randomized, double-blinded, placebo-controlled trial. McCann D, Barrett A, Cooper A, Crumpler D, Dalen L, Grimshaw K, Kitchin E, Lok K, Porteous L, Prince E, Sonuga-Barke E, Warner JO, Stevenson J. *Lancet*. 2007 Nov 3;370(9598):1560-7. Erratum in: *Lancet*. 2007 Nov 3;370(9598):1542.

6 Ageloglou, Christodoulos. *Elder Paisios of the Holy Mountain*. Holy Mountain: S.n., 1998, p. 141.

7 http://www.cnn.com/2014/03/06/health/who-sugar-guidelines/ [accessed February 18, 2015]

8 *Pharmacol Biochem Behav*. 2010 Nov; 97(1):101-6. doi: 10.1016/j.pbb.2010.02.012. Epub 2010 Feb 26. High-fructose corn syrup causes characteristics of obesity in rats: increased body weight, body fat and triglyceride levels. Bocarsly ME, Powell ES, Avena NM, Hoebel BG

9 http://www.princeton.edu/main/news/archive/S26/91/22K07/ [accessed September 1, 2014]

10 http://www.ncbi.nlm.nih.gov/pubmed/23850261 [accessed March 3, 2015]

11 http://www.sas.upenn.edu/sasalum/newsltr/fall97/rozin.html [accessed September 1, 2014]

12 http://www.eurekalert.org/pub_releases/2012-05/lu-hdl051112.php [accessed March 3, 2015]

13 Schmemann, Alexander. *For the Life of the World: Sacraments and Orthodoxy.* Crestwood, NY: St. Vladimir's Seminary Press, 1973, p. 17.

14 Tracy, Kathleen. *Ellen: The Real Story of Ellen DeGeneres.* Pinnacle, 2005, p. 326.

15 http://www.northwestmedicalcenter.com/northwest-medical-center/health-library/most-adults-are-members-of-clean-plate-club-36174.aspx [accessed September 10, 2014]

16 Archimandrite Dositheos. *Greek Monastery Cookery.* Epralofos S.A., 2003, p. 331.

17 Wansink, Brian. *Mindless Eating: Why We Eat More Than We Think.* Bantam, 2010, p. 68.

18 Wansink, *op. cit.*, p. 67.

19 http://orthodoxinfo.com/praxis/rules.aspx [accessed February 21, 2015]

20 http://massreport.com/new-study-fasting-may-regenerate-the-entire-immune-system/ [accessed February 22, 2015]

21 Spidlik, Tomas. *Drinking from the Hidden Fountain: A Patristic Breviary.* Ancient Wisdom for Today's World (Cistercian Studies). Cistercian Publications, 1993, p. 69.

22 http://www.dailymotion.com/video/xz2fwb_the-truth-about-exercise_lifestyle [accessed February 28, 2015]

23 http://atenist2.rssing.com/chan-1984859/all_p156.html [accessed February 28, 2015]

24 http://www.newscientist.com/article/dn24002-poor-sleep-makes-food-more-appealing.html#.VJU6914BE [accessed March 7, 2015]

25 http://www.bloomberg.com/news/2014-01-07/bedroom-invading-smartphones-jumble-body-s-sleep-rhythms.html [accessed March 7, 2015].

26 Spidlik, *op. cit.*, p. 80.

27 Ageloglou, *op. cit.*, pp. 43–44.

28 http://greatergood.berkeley.edu/article/item/kindness_makes_you_happy_and_happiness_makes_you_kind [accessed March 7, 2015]

29 http://www.americamagazine.org/content/all-things/centering-prayer-contemplative-practice-21st-century [accessed March 8, 2015]

Also, Sperry, Len. *Spirituality in Clinical Practice: Theory and Practice of Spiritually Oriented Psychotherapy*. 2nd Edition. Routledge, 2011.

About the Author

Rita Madden, MPH, RDN, is the nutrition director for Mediterranean Wellness, a company that focuses on sensible weight loss/management and chronic disease prevention/management. She completed her graduate work in public-health nutrition at Loma Linda University. She has a podcast on the subject of food, health, and the Eastern Orthodox Faith on Ancient Faith Radio. She is also a member of the Orthodox Speakers Bureau, through which she conducts workshops on this subject matter on a nationwide level. Rita is passionate about this subject matter and is devoted to helping people form a healthy relationship with food.